How to Know Your Agreement Will Work
Without Triggering It

BUY-SELL
AGREEMENTS
for Closely Held and Family Business Owners

Z. Christopher Mercer, ASA, CFA, ABAR

PRAISE FOR
BUY-SELL AGREEMENTS
for Closely Held and Family Business Owners

Buy-Sell Agreements for Closely Held and Family Business Owners presents this most important topic in an understandable fashion. The book will assist business owners in getting their ownership affairs in order before the issue of a buy-out erupts, as it often does, at the least opportune time, damaging the business and the relationships among the owners.

Roger J. Grabowski, ASA
Managing Director, Duff & Phelps

This is the business owner's self-defense manual. Reading it could be the most cost-effective hour or two you've ever invested. Don't dare sign a buy-sell agreement until you've read and pondered the questions posed in this book. Your life('s work) may depend on it!

Stephan R. Leimberg
Chief Executive Officer and Publisher, Leimberg Information Services, Inc.

Having advised clients on buy-sell agreements for more than 30 years, both from a legal and life insurance funding perspective, I have seen the financially devastating consequences of poor planning. Chris Mercer's book is the best treatise on this topic and is a must-read for any attorney, financial/insurance planner, or business owner working on buy-sell agreements.

Kelly Finnell, J.D., CLU, AIF°
*Author, The ESOP Coach: Using ESOPs in Ownership Succession Planning
President, Executive Financial Services, Inc.*

As a lawyer who works mostly with closely held and family-owned businesses, I've seen many buy-sell agreements, and I've drafted my share of them. I can say unequivocally that this is the most useful analysis of the subject I've encountered. The book is relatively compact, but it's not in the least superficial or truncated. On the contrary, Chris Mercer has produced a uniquely practical handbook for business owners and their advisors which is thorough and comprehensive, but at the same time is clear, straightforward, and understandable. In direct and non-technical terms, Mercer thoughtfully explores the pros and cons of competing approaches, and unflinchingly expresses his specific recommendations. Anyone who owns or advises a privately owned business needs to read this book.

Jared Kaplan
Senior Counsel, McDermott Will & Emery

A must-read for business owners and their advisors. The book identifies and explains all the issues of buy-sell agreements in clear, understandable terms.

Gerald A. Shanker, CPA/ABV
Founding Member, Kreinces Rollins & Shanker, LLC

This book is very well-researched, easy to understand, and contains numerous helpful examples. It reminds us in great detail how many of the components of a buy-sell agreement cause more problems than they solve. I particularly liked the charts that succinctly presented the advantages and disadvantages of the important elements of a good buy-sell agreement. Also, this book is not just for valuation analysts. Business owners should read it too. It is also a must-read for CPAs, financial planners, attorneys, and anyone else who advises business owners.

James R. Hitchner, CPA/ABV/CFF, ASA
Managing Director, Financial Valuation Advisors
Chief Executive Officer, Valuation Products and Services
President, Financial Consulting Group

The biggest problem with a buy-sell agreement is it is never looked at once it is signed. Based on today's circumstances, will it act the way you expected? Most don't. Chris Mercer's book will give you big picture ideas without legal mumbo jumbo.

Larry H. Colin
Author/Producer, FAMILY, Inc.

Your buy-sell agreement is the most important business document you are likely to ever create. It is in every owner's direct interest to make certain it works exactly as intended – before it is intended to be triggered. Chris Mercer's previous book on buy-sell agreements is the "industry standard," and we recommend it to the hundreds of business advisors who belong to our exit planning organization. This new book is likewise destined to be a "standard" for business owners. It is premised on the criticality of establishing an accurate business valuation regardless of the circumstances which trigger an owner's departure. In a straightforward and easily understood style, it describes what owners need to do today to prevent unintended, and perhaps financially ruinous, consequences tomorrow.

John Brown
Author, How To Run Your Business So You Can Leave It In Style
President, Business Executives International

As the founder of one successful business and current participant in a family-owned bank, I thought I was something of a veteran when it comes to business. When I read Chris Mercer's *Buy-Sell Agreements for Closely Held and Family Business Owners*, I realized that there is still a great deal to learn. The book is an in-depth and candid look at buy-sell agreements, which we all have and seldom think about. What I realized in reading the book is that the things that we don't think about naturally, without help like in Chris' new book, are the things that can really go wrong.

Kenneth B. Lenoir
Executive Vice President, Evolve Bank & Trust Company
(former Founder, Chairman, and CEO of First Mercantile Trust Company)

As a "recovering" tax attorney and a current advisor to many family businesses, I found myself chuckling as I read Chris Mercer's book, *Buy-Sell Agreements for Closely Held and Family Business Owners*. The chuckles were a bit rueful, however, for Chris Mercer says straight out what I seldom could say to my clients – that they were letting themselves be intimidated by the complexities of buy-sell planning into passivity on the single most important agreement they may ever sign. I imagine many lawyers will buy copies of this book and use it as homework for their clients.

Not only is it accurate and amazingly readable, but it also places the focus exactly where it should be – on the owner and his or her willingness to address tough issues head on. Many business owners would rather talk about a prenuptial agreement with a fiancée than a buy-sell agreement with his partner. After all, discussing the future dissolution of a successful working relationship requires talking about death, disability, divorce, and, toughest of all, whether we will be able to afford to buy the other out at a "fair" price.

My advice to professionals is to give the owners of a closely held business this book and several days to read it. The next meeting will be more productive, more realistic, and there will be no talk about "just" preparing a "standard" buy-sell agreement. The book imparts two great lessons. First, there is no such thing as a "standard" buy-sell agreement. Second, and even more striking, defining a "fair price" to govern far into the future is far more challenging than the owners ever imagined. This last lesson comes home with a vengeance since Chris Mercer is a skilled business appraiser and his writing shines a light into the murk of valuation language and options. Indeed, the most illuminating parts of the book deal with the logical quagmire amateurs can sink into when trying to define "value" without the (very necessary) aid of a qualified appraiser to lead the discussion and calculation of valuation throughout the life of the agreement.

Stephen G. Salley
Senior Partner, GenSpring Family Offices

For shareholders of closely held businesses, this book presents a comprehensive and understandable discussion of the essential elements of buy-sell agreements and how to correct deficiencies that commonly occur. We have followed the author's very appropriate advice to make sure you have an ironclad, foolproof system to keep the price current by getting an annual appraisal.

W. J. "Bill" Rankin, CPA
Chief Financial Officer, Blue Bell Creameries, L.P.

Chris Mercer has seen the world of valuation through many eyes. His experience and broad insights to the process of valuation adds a dimension that few can compare. He brings knowledge from a combination of multi-business landscapes and industries. This is a must-read for family-owned and closely held business entities. No one is more qualified to write on these subjects than Chris Mercer.

Alan Hughes
President, Clear Processes, LLC
(Retired Division Manager, Dealer Development, John Deere Co.)

A buy-sell agreement is one of the most critical agreements in any closely held business. It must be done right to avoid serious disputes among business owners when one of the owners dies, quits or is terminated, becomes disabled or divorced, or gets into financial trouble. Chris Mercer does a masterful job in *Buy-Sell Agreements for Closely Held and Family Business Owners* of discussing the key issues in a thoughtful and easy-to-read manner. With more than 30 years of expertise in the field, Chris explains why the failure to have a solid buy-sell agreement may be devastating to a business and its owners, and provides very practical tips on how you can greatly improve your buy-sell agreement.

Nathaniel L. Doliner
Shareholder, Carlton Fields, P.A.

In a word, "Wow!" *Buy-Sell Agreements for Closely Held and Family Business Owners* contains the most in-depth discussion of the "whys" of buy-sell agreements that I've ever read. Chris Mercer has focused his laser beam mind upon probably the hardest and most under-served area of business planning: buy-sell agreements. Read this book!

L. Paul Hood, Jr.
Attorney at Law

Chris Mercer has the unparalleled capacity and intellectual capital to drill deeper on this topic than anyone. His perspective and premises are sound and the sub-topics covered on buy-sell agreements will give you the entire spectrum. I would not think about going into buy-sell agreement negotiations without reading this book again, cover-to-cover, the night before. Don't miss this one – it will only cost you if you don't read it!

Don Hutson
Speaker and Co-author of the
Wall Street Journal and New York Times #1 Best-Seller,
The One Minute Entrepreneur
Chief Executive Officer, U.S. Learning

The concept of regular (annual) valuations to update buy-sell agreements is really useful. As a consultant helping businesses focus on strategy and growth and having been involved in a buy-sell agreement dispute as a business owner, I can attest to the great value of incorporating this concept into the governance of the business. Not only does it help business owners focus on business value creation, but when used regularly as part of buy-sell agreement updates, it helps the business keep these essential agreements updated and current. This has the benefit of increasing owner/partner alignment by avoiding unpleasant disappointments or disagreements about business value in the future.

Dr. Brian Cassell, DVM
Founder and Managing Partner, Dynamic Veterinary Concepts
Executive Director, MOON, An Innovation Veterinary Collaborative

How to Know Your Agreement Will Work
Without Triggering It

BUY-SELL
AGREEMENTS
for Closely Held and Family Business Owners

Z. Christopher Mercer, ASA, CFA, ABAR

BUY-SELL AGREEMENTS
for Closely Held and Family Business Owners
How to Know Your Agreement Will Work Without Triggering It

ISBN: 978-0-9825364-3-8

Peabody Publishing LP
5100 Poplar Avenue
Suite 2600
Memphis, Tennessee 38137
901.685.210 (p)

for Ashley,
the love of my life

Table of Contents

PART III: VALUATION PROCESS BUY-SELL AGREEMENTS

Acknowledgements

This book was sent to a number of friends and colleagues for early reviews. Special thanks go to Steve Leimberg, Roger Grabowski, Jim Hitchner, Gerald Shanker, Will Frazier, Curt Kimball, and Nat Doliner, who went above and beyond with their helpful suggestions for improving the book and for helping me eliminate misstatements and inconsistencies. The book is far better as result of your reviews.

To all those who read the book and provided the words of praise, thank you. You encouraged me in this effort.

Tom Deans, author of *Every Family's Business: 12 Common Sense Questions to Protect Your Wealth*, has been a strong supporter of this project for many months and has provided invaluable counsel. He challenged me to make this book as non-technical as possible. A conversation with him triggered the idea for the "Pete and Sam" dialogue that introduces each chapter. And thank you, Tom, for providing the foreword to this book.

Every book has to have a title – even if it's a long one. This one is the result of a brainstorming session with Barbara Walters Price, who has been instrumental in completing, not only this book, but every book I've written to date.

My friends and colleagues at Mercer Capital have helped in many ways. Thanks to Matt Crow and Tim Lee for their ongoing help and encouragement. Thanks to Todd Lowe for tirelessly supporting me in this project and all others. Special thanks to Matt Washburn for the cover design and the look of the book.

I bring to this book project the experiences of having read, worked on, or interpreted hundreds of buy-sell agreements from valuation and business perspectives. I thank the clients who have allowed me the privilege of this never-ending laboratory for learning.

Michael Graber, who edited my book *The Integrated Theory of Business Valuation*, and his wonderful staff at Southern Growth Studios, did a masterful job of helping me say what I really meant to say in clearer, more concise, and more understandable prose. Thank you.

Most importantly, thank you to my wife, Ashley, for her patience with me and for her encouragement in bringing this book across the finish line. She shared me with this book on many occasions. However, during our "vacation" at our place in Destin, Florida during the month of June, her patience took on new meaning!

Our children, Katherine, Katherine, Margaret, and Zeno, keep my life more than interesting and provide continuing motivation to keep on keeping on. My grown daughter, Amanda, has become an excellent sounding board. Thanks!

Finally, where I have failed to listen to the good advice provided to me by so many, any remaining errors, misspellings, misstatements, or other gotchas are my responsibility.

August 10, 2010
Memphis, Tennessee

FOREWORD

Chris Mercer's most important book to date on buy-sell agreements offers business owners and their advisors a straightforward, practical tool for planning the ownership transfer of a firm.

But what is certain to become the definitive book on buy-sell agreements is so much more than a technical compendium.

Although Chris wrote this book in a refreshing, and at times, humorous tone, readers can't help but wonder how many business owners he has witnessed during his long career who failed to plan for their business's inevitable transition. The value of this book lies in the seemingly endless examples of business owners who destroyed their own wealth. The recurring theme is consistently ill-conceived or outdated buy-sell agreements – or worse, no buy-sell agreement at all.

As a professional business valuator, as an acknowledged expert in his field, as an expert witness, Chris has occupied a front-row seat in courtrooms and boardrooms; one is left with the feeling that what he saw was often disheartening. Maybe having watched so many families twist in the wind and fight publicly over the question – "what is this business worth?" – after the owners' father, mother, brother, or sister died, took its toll.

If it did, then surely everyone who reads this book will emerge the beneficiary of this author's professional odyssey. His choosing to share his personal insights on an age-old problem – "how do I place a value on my business in the event I am divorced, disabled, or dead?" – is no small challenge. That Chris has written such an entertaining book on such an emotional (some would argue tedious and perplexing) subject is significant.

This book is as much about protecting owners and families as it is about protecting wealth. It's as much about protecting a business owner's legacy as it is about maximizing shareholder value. The paradox of a buy-sell agreement is that the beneficiary is often not present to see the fruits of wise planning accrue. The process of crafting and revisiting a buy-sell agreement requires introspection and self-awareness, making it the ultimate testimonial of the savvy business owner who gives lasting purpose and meaning to the wealth he or she creates. Alas, this is a book about family legacy.

If ever in history there was a moment when business owners required this book and its message, now is that time. In this country the leading edge of Baby Boomers – those born in 1949 – are entering their sixties, and they are business owners in record numbers. How the greatest wealth-creating generation in the history of mankind plans for their "last deal" will reveal as much about them as individuals as it does about the collective values of an entire generation.

If family is as important as most business owners say it is, advisors will buy this book in bulk and distribute it to their business owner clients. Advisors will use this book as a wake-up call to business owners who flirt with calamitous risks to themselves and their families by ignoring the importance of reviewing their buy-sell agreement.

Making wealth and protecting it to fund long, fulfilling retirements and the future prosperity of succeeding generations doesn't happen by accident. But it can and will start with business owners reading this thoughtfully crafted book and zeroing in on what's most important – family.

Tom Deans, Ph.D.
Author, Every Family's Business

PREFACE

Every successful closely held or family-owned business with two or more owners has a buy-sell agreement – and if it doesn't, it should.

Buy-sell agreements govern how ownership will change hands if and when something significant, often called a trigger event, happens to one or more of the owners. These agreements are intended to ensure the remaining owners control the outcome during critical transitions. They specify what happens to the ownership interest of a fellow owner who dies or otherwise departs the business, and mandate that a departing owner be paid reasonably for his or her interest in the business.

Buy-sell agreements *are supposed to work* by:

- Providing a market for the shares (or partnership interests or member interests) in the event an owner dies or has to leave the company.

- Establishing the price and terms for the market so future transactions under the buy-sell agreement occur in an orderly and reasonable fashion.

- Specifying or otherwise assuring financing (or life insurance or cash) is available to acquire shares in the event an owner departs.

Unfortunately, based on my experience working with closely held and family businesses for more than 30 years, most buy-sell agreements won't accomplish their objectives in an orderly and reasonable fashion. My first book on the subject, *Buy-Sell Agreements: Ticking Time Bombs or Reasonable Resolutions?* (2007) addressed the problem primarily from the viewpoint of business advisors.

This book was based on reading many buy-sell agreements, since most of the companies I have valued have or had buy-sell agreements. I have been involved with many buy-sell agreements following trigger events. Trigger events, as we will see, are those (mostly) bad things that cause buy-sell agreements to be put into operation, including death, disability, firings, and numerous others.

We will talk in this book about valuation processes involving one, two, or three business appraisers for determining the price for buy-sell agreement transactions. I have been the first or second appraiser selected by the sides in many valuation processes. And I have been the third appraiser selected by the first two appraisers in many more situations.

These experiences all inform my understanding of buy-sell agreements and how they work from business and valuation perspectives. In addition, I have personally been a party to several buy-sell agreements at Mercer Capital and at other companies where I have been an investor.

This book, *Buy-Sell Agreements for Closely Held and Family Business Owners: How to Know Your Agreement Will Work Without Triggering It*, is written for all business owners who have or will have buy-sell agreements for their companies. I have seen enough explosions following the triggering of buy-sell agreements to know that badly crafted agreements can be disastrous for all involved. However, you can know in advance your buy-sell agreement will work – and it doesn't have to be triggered to find out. This book explains how.

Understand the Dangers of Your Current Agreement

Buy-sell agreements have three basic types of pricing mechanisms.

Fixed-price agreements. You and the other owners agree on a price and set that price in the agreement.

FIXED-PRICE AGREEMENTS

Description

- You and the other owner(s) agreed on a price.

- That price of your agreement is likely years out of date.

- There are three possibilities regarding the price you set:

  - The value today is lower, perhaps far lower, than the realistic value.

  - The value today is higher, perhaps far higher, than the realistic value.

  - The value is the same as it was back then.

> You haven't agreed on a way to update the price.

Realities Seldom Discussed

- If the value is unrealistically low, you are betting that the other guy will die first and you'll get to buy at the low price.

- If the value is unrealistically high, you are betting that you'll be the one to leave the business so you and your family can benefit.

- The other guy(s) are making just the opposite bets.

> Why take a chance that you'll be on the wrong end of that bet?

Formula agreements. You and the other owners agree on a formula to calculate the price.

FORMULA PRICE AGREEMENTS

Description

- You and the other owner(s) established a formula to calculate price.

- Chances are, no one has calculated it lately.

- Chances are, it can give an unreasonable result now.

- Combined with changes in the company and the industry:

    - The formula price may be higher than a realistic value today.

    - The formula price may be lower than a realistic value today.

    - The formula price is realistic today.

> **You haven't agreed on ways to make necessary/appropriate adjustments.**

Realities Seldom Discussed

- If the value is unrealistically low, you are betting that the other guy will die first and you'll get to buy at the low price.

- If the value is unrealistically high, you are betting that you'll be the one to leave the business so you and your family can benefit.

- The other guy(s) are making just the opposite bets.

> **Why take a chance that you'll be on the wrong end of that bet?**

Valuation process agreements. You and the other owners agree that if the buy-sell agreement is triggered, you will bring in one or more business appraisers to determine the price.

VALUATION PROCESS AGREEMENTS

Description

- ◉ You and the other owners agreed to let business appraisers set the price for your agreement if and when it is triggered.

- ◉ No one has the foggiest idea what will happen or what the price will be.

- ◉ No one knows what "kind of value" the appraiser will provide:

  - It could be the value of an illiquid interest.

  - It could be the value of the entire enterprise pro rata to ownership.

  - It could be reasonable and what you thought you agreed to.

  - It might not be reasonable and what you thought you agreed to.

> No one will know until the end of a lengthy and uncertain process what the outcome will be.

Realities Seldom Discussed

- ◉ You are betting that the ultimate price will be favorable (or at least reasonable) for you.

- ◉ The other owners are betting that the ultimate price will be favorable (or at least reasonable) for them.

- ◉ The company is betting that the process will work and that the price set will be affordable.

> Everyone is betting and someone will lose.

Your company's buy-sell agreement has one (or possibly a combination) of these pricing mechanisms. This reality will hold true whether the agreement is between the owners and the company (an entity agreement) or between you and your fellow owners (a cross-purchase agreement).

A Word to the Wise

The bottom line is whether your buy-sell agreement has a fixed-price, is a formula agreement, or contains a valuation process, chances are that you, the other owners, and your company are in for a surprise when it is triggered.

Buy-Sell Agreements for Closely Held and Family Business Owners is written so you can prevent your flawed agreement from exploding and harming you, your fellow owners, all of your families, and even the company itself – and you can do this without triggering the agreement.

How to Read this Book

The cost of this book is insignificant. What is important is your time. If you invest the time to read it, I promise you will gain understanding and learn tools to eliminate this danger from your business and your life.

I recommend that you read this book aggressively.

- ◉ Highlight relevant facts or issues for further study.

- ◉ Raise questions or make comments in the margins to focus your thinking about buy-sell agreements generally, or about your agreement specifically.

- ◉ If you have an existing buy-sell agreement, read it in conjunction with this book. If you have a partnership or LLC, the buy-sell provision may be included in the basic agreement. Raise questions in your agreement and add to your notes. The *Buy-Sell Agreement Audit Checklist*, written for use with this book, is available for you to download at www.buysellagreementsonline.com. Order the checklist, which sells for $19.95, and enter the discount code "FREE" to download the checklist at no cost.

⊚ If you are initiating a buy-sell agreement at the time you are reading this book, make notes relating to your situation. Then, consolidate your notes on the *Buy-Sell Agreement Audit Checklist* before discussing them with legal counsel or other business advisors. If they are participating in the process with you, work through the checklist together.

⊚ Share the book with your fellow shareholders and use the outline and the *Buy-Sell Agreement Audit Checklist* to facilitate the discussion.

⊚ Have a valuation professional read your buy-sell agreement from valuation and business perspectives and identify potential problems.

⊚ Have your financial planner or tax attorney read the buy-sell agreement to determine if it is consistent with your personal estate planning.

Use this book as an active tool to help you, your lawyers, and other advisors craft workable agreements. Is your buy-sell agreement a ticking time bomb? Or will it provide a reasonable resolution to the future transactions it contemplates? The problem is up to you to resolve.

PART I

Why Your Buy-Sell Agreement Won't Work

Chapter One

Your Buy-Sell Agreement Won't Work

Let's talk about buy-sell agreements. In particular, let's talk about your buy-sell agreement. As part of our conversation, you can listen in on a discussion I am having with a business owner named Sam. I will act as his consultant, Pete, which was my father's nickname for me.

Sam owns 40% of a successful closely held company. He and his long-time business partner set up a buy-sell agreement when they started their business almost 20 years ago. My purpose in talking to Sam is to help him understand the actual issues he has with his buy-sell agreement and to encourage him, together with the other owners of the business, to take action. Sam, like you in all likelihood, passively assumes that his buy-sell agreement will work. In reality, it's like a time bomb.

Pete:	**"Sam, I just buried a small bomb in your yard. It isn't large enough to kill you, your wife, or another member of your family, but it would certainly maim you or them if one of you stepped on it."**
Sam:	"Where is it?"
Pete:	**"I'm not going to tell you where it is. But don't worry. Chances are it is so well-hidden that no one will ever step on it."**

Sam:	"What do you mean, 'chances are'? That's a chance I can't take! If it were just me it would be one thing, but you're talking about hurting my wife and family!"
Pete:	**"Like I said, don't worry. Maybe no one will ever step on it. Maybe it will never explode."**
Sam:	"You must be crazy! I'll bring in a bomb squad and dig up the entire yard to get rid of it!"
Pete:	**"Now Sam, you know I'm just kidding about the bomb. However, your buy-sell agreement might very well be a ticking time bomb and you just don't know it. How about taking some time to talk about your buy-sell agreement – say, dinner tomorrow night?"**
Sam:	"Sounds good to me. See you then."

If you knew there was a bomb in your yard that could harm you and your family, you would not stop until you found it and had it disarmed.

If you are like most owners of private businesses, your investment in the business represents a substantial portion of your net worth – maybe almost all of it. So when I talk about a bomb in the company yard, I'm talking about a bomb that can determine the timing of and return you get on your largest investment.

There is no bomb in your yard, but you almost certainly have one lurking within the words on the pages of your buy-sell agreement. If you haven't done anything to fix it, you and your fellow owners need the equivalent of the bomb squad. By inaction, you have placed yourself, your families, and your company in real danger. This analogy is the clearest way I can communicate to you the importance of disarming this bomb before it explodes.

The conversation continues at dinner the next evening.

Pete:	**"Sam, how many owners are there in your business?"**

Sam:	"We have four owners. My long-time partner, George, and I own 80% of the business between us. William and Don, who we brought in about 10 years ago, now own 10% each."

Pete:	**"How long has it been since you had a conversation with George about your buy-sell agreement?"**

Sam:	"It has been quite a few years."

Pete:	**"And how about with William and Don?"**

Sam:	"Well, we never really talked about it other than to tell them they had to sign the agreement if they became owners."

Pete:	**"Sam, I can't tell you how important it is for you guys to talk to each other about it."**

Sam:	"I know. You keep saying that. But it is just hard to talk about the buy-sell agreement. Things get kind of testy when the topic comes up, so we just keep putting off talking about it."

The Problem Lies with the Owners

A buy-sell agreement is an agreement between a company and its shareholders. For purposes of simplicity, we typically refer to business enterprises as "the company" or "the corporation" in the text. Business owners will generally be referred to as "shareholders" or "owners."

Buy-sell agreements are prevalent throughout the corporate world. They are common when businesses have multiple shareholders, partners, or joint venture participants. Virtually every company of any size with two or more shareholders has a buy-sell agreement. They are important business and legal documents. Your company has a buy-sell agreement – or needs one – otherwise you probably wouldn't be reading this book.

Buy-sell agreements are too often overlooked by the owners. They almost always get triggered unexpectedly. Who expects to die, to be fired, or to become disabled? These things happen to other folks – until one of them happens to you.

Chances are, your buy-sell agreement is flawed and will not work like you think it will or should work. You may think this is a bold or presumptuous statement since you know I have not seen your agreement. Nevertheless, it is likely a true statement, as you will see. My perspective is that of a businessman (and business owner) and a valuation expert who has read many buy-sell agreements, who has participated in many processes where buy-sell agreements have been triggered, and who has been a party to several buy-sell agreements personally.

Most of the problems in buy-sell agreements relate to business objectives considered (or not) and the valuation mechanisms or processes found (or found lacking) in them.

I'm not a lawyer and am not blaming lawyers for likely problems in your agreement. On the contrary, most lawyers really attempt to work with their clients to develop good buy-sell agreements. Too often, in fact, what may have been a good buy-sell agreement when first written becomes obsolete with the passage of time.

As Pogo famously said, "We have met the enemy and he is us."

The blame for most of the business and/or valuation problems with buy-sell agreements almost always rest on the shoulders of company owners.

- Only the owners can state their business objectives.
- Only the owners can negotiate with fellow owners regarding personal objectives and desires.
- And only the owners can articulate what they want to happen when those future events contemplated by their buy-sell agreements actually happen.

Most of us think or act like nothing can ever happen to us. But things happen to us all, and things will happen to you and/or your fellow shareholders. Remember, bad things do happen to good people.

Your company's buy-sell agreement will determine a number of critical things:

- Who can be a shareholder and who can or will buy shares under the agreement.
- What will happen when trigger events occur.
- What price will be paid and how (under what terms) it will be paid.

And finally, the agreement determines how much money *the other owner(s)* will receive when something happens to them. After all, nothing will ever happen to you – until it does!

How Buy-Sell Agreements Come Into Existence

Business lawyers and business persons with any experience know companies and their owners need buy-sell agreements to protect the interests of the corporation and their shareholders. However, as important as buy-sell agreements are, many are created almost as an afterthought, particularly from the viewpoint of shareholders in private businesses.

When transactions are consummated or companies are created, the shareholders tend to think their work is complete. After all, they have agreed on the economics of the investment and their relative ownership positions. They should be able to get down to business.

At this point, an experienced business attorney says to the shareholders, "Now, we have to put a buy-sell agreement in place. You do want to take care of things appropriately if one of you should die, don't you? You need to agree on a buy-sell agreement to determine what happens if one of you quits, is fired, retires, dies, or is disabled. These are things that can happen."

The attorney goes on to say, "And you want to control who you do business with in the future, don't you? The most likely way to do that is to prepare a right of first refusal agreement. So let's talk about the important issues this raises for your consideration and agreement."

At this moment, the pace of communication between the attorneys and the owners frequently begins to slow. Investors are weary of negotiations and ready to move on with their business proposition. They typically don't want to spend any more money on legal or other professional fees, and many definitely don't want to talk about their own mortalities, the potential of future fallouts, retirements, or disabilities. They also know that a real discussion of a buy-sell agreement would be difficult and potentially divisive based on one or more actual or potential opposing characteristics within the shareholder group.

POTENTIAL OPPOSING SHAREHOLDER CHARACTERISTICS
THAT MAKE DISCUSSING BUY-SELL AGREEMENTS DIFFICULT

Characteristic	Shareholder 1	Shareholder 2
Age	Younger	Older
Ownership	Noncontrolling	Controlling
Involvement	Active	Inactive
Personal Outlook	Optimistic	Pessimistic
Investment Type	Sweat Equity	Real Money
Investment Amount	Smaller	Larger to Much Larger
Personal Guaranties	None	Substantial

FIGURE 1

Then, someone volunteers to the attorney and other owners, "We've all been in business, and we know what buy-sell agreements are all about. You have one in your word processor, don't you?"

The attorney replies, "Yes, we have several templates that provide a basis for discussion about the particular needs and circumstances of your business and its ownership. But we need to adapt the template to this situation." The attorney is attempting to deliver an extremely important message.

Nevertheless, the shareholder replies, "You've been here the entire time we've been putting this deal together and you know us, so just give us a basic buy-sell agreement so we'll have one. You have a boilerplate version, don't you?" Then, he tempts fate: "There'll never be a problem, anyway!"

Your attorney drafts an agreement (or agreements if there is an accompanying right of first refusal to be put in place) subject to the review and approval of all of the parties. The shareholders glance at them and sign the dotted line. The agreements go into the corporate records and personal lockboxes until trigger events happen – and trigger events will almost certainly occur.

A good number of buy-sell agreements are also initiated in the context of gift and estate tax planning for owners. While buy-sell agreements can facilitate such planning, their development with gift and estate tax aspects is no less difficult than the process outlined above. Competent tax and corporate counsel will be required.

The Solution Lies with the Owners

If there are problems with your buy-sell agreement, now is the time to identify and address them. Get your buy-sell agreement out of the safe or filing cabinet or attorney's office and keep it with you for reference as you read this book.

The solution for the problems with your buy-sell agreement lies with you and the other owners.

- Think about why your company has a buy-sell agreement and what it is helping the shareholders to accomplish.

- Think about your own personal objectives and concerns about the agreement.

- Talk with the other owner(s) and with appropriate company officers and directors.

- Follow the advice of this book and begin a thorough review of your buy-sell agreement from business, valuation, and legal perspectives.

- Engage appropriate professionals to help define and refine corporate business objectives, as well as the intersections between corporate and personal objectives.

The bottom line is that the time for action is now. The company and all parties will be bound by what I call "the words on the pages" of the agreement. Once it is triggered, it is too late to fix anything because the interests of the parties will have diverged, rendering it almost impossible for them to find agreement over issues that arise.

THIS BOOK IS FOR YOU

Private ownership of businesses is a wonderful thing. We can own, operate, and enjoy the fruits of our investments of capital and labor through our businesses.

If you own 100% of a business, you can do anything you want to with it. You can operate it and eventually sell it if you wish. That would be a good thing. Or, you can run it into the ground. You can run it until you drop from the saddle. If you die, you can leave it to your spouse or your children – even if they don't have the foggiest idea what to do with it. Or, you can leave it to your creditors. None of these may be a good plan, but you can do it.

The fact is, by the time most businesses get to be of significant size or have significant value, they have multiple owners. And your business probably has more than one owner. You are likely interested in this book on buy-sell agreements because of that.

Buy-sell agreements are simple in concept. They set the terms for buying and selling corporate shares when certain things happen. But many believe that most of the things buy-sell agreements are designed to protect against will never happen to us. And if we don't actually believe it, we act as if we do.

This is precisely why this book about buy-sell agreements is for you, your fellow shareholders and directors, and your company, whether it is a corporation, a partnership, a limited liability corporation, or anything else.

My challenge to you is to use it as a tool to prevent your buy-sell agreement from exploding on you and your other owners. You can know your buy-sell agreement will work without triggering it.

Chapter Two

Begin at the Beginning

Pete:	"Sam, I really enjoyed dinner the other night."
Sam:	"I did as well, Pete. Thanks for picking up the tab."
Pete:	"It was my pleasure. I'm glad you agreed to meet with me today. When we began to talk about your buy-sell agreement the other night, you seemed a little worried and anxious about it. So here we are. We've both set aside a few hours, so let's see what we can accomplish."
Sam:	"Sounds good to me!"
Pete:	"At dinner, you reacted pretty strongly when I told you your buy-sell agreement was a ticking time bomb that needed attention now."
Sam:	"You haven't even read it yet! Don't worry, I brought a couple of copies of the agreement as you suggested."
Pete:	"Great! You know, I hate to say it, but I don't even have to read your agreement to know that something is wrong with it. I just don't know what at this point."
Sam:	"Well, what might that be?"
Pete:	"Well, let me ask a few questions first."

Begin with the End in Mind

In his durable bestseller, *Seven Habits of Highly Effective People,* Stephen Covey suggests we begin with the end in mind.

> "Begin with the End in Mind" means to begin each day, task or project with a clear vision of your desired direction and destination, and then continue by flexing your proactive muscles to make things happen.

The *end in mind* at the beginning of this book is to encourage, cajole, push, or otherwise embarrass you into focusing on your buy-sell agreement so you can stop it from being the ticking time bomb in your personal or company yard. Workable buy-sell agreements that will provide reasonable valuation processes and valuations following specified trigger events is the goal. If you share this goal, start with the follow questions.

Beginning Questions

We begin our investigation of buy-sell agreements by asking six questions and offering preliminary comments for you to think about:

- **Who** are the parties to your buy-sell agreement?

  - Normally, this will be you, the other shareholders, and your company.

  - Often, with the passage of time, new shareholders do not become subject to agreements, either through oversight or a reluctance to discuss the issues with new owners.

- **What** is your buy-sell agreement designed to accomplish?

  - Most agreements are designed to specify a reasonable way for future transactions in your company's stock to be accomplished when certain things happen in the future.

- This worthwhile objective is not met when many buy-sell agreements are created.

- **When** will your buy-sell agreement come into play?

  - Most agreements are set to operate when certain unpleasant things happen, such as deaths, disabilities, or firings.

  - One thing all agreements have in common is they relate to future events and future circumstances that most of us don't want to think about in the present.

  - Another common factor is neither you nor anyone else knows what will cause an agreement to be triggered.

  - Importantly, when agreements are created, no one knows when they will come into play.

- **Where** will your buy-sell agreement work?

  - You might still be running the business, or not working in the business at all.

  - You might be the buying shareholder or the selling shareholder (or you might be the dearly departed partner whose family is relying upon the buy-sell agreement to work as it was intended).

  - Where you will be and what role you will play when the buy-sell agreement is triggered is important as you consider how your agreement will operate.

⊚ **Why** do you have a buy-sell agreement?

- Everyone knows instinctively that it is difficult to reach an agreement about important financial matters after something bad happens. At that point, the proverbial ox is in the ditch. That's why people prepare wills – so their children won't fight over things or assets when they die.

- Your buy-sell agreement should be designed so you and the other shareholders can reach agreement now, before anything happens.

- Chances are you have a buy-sell agreement because your attorney or another advisor told you it was necessary to have one.

⊚ **How** will your buy-sell agreement operate?

- Buy-sell agreements are designed, in theory at least, to determine the price at which future transactions will occur when those bad things we don't want to talk about happen. They also establish the process by which that price is established, and the terms under which future transactions will occur.

- In reality, unless your agreement has previously been triggered, chances are you have no idea how it will operate. Don't feel badly about this. Almost no one does. But motivate yourself to find out!

If all of these questions were answered appropriately for the majority of buy-sell agreements, then we would not be writing about them. *The blunt reality is that the questions above are too often left unanswered or are poorly addressed in the great majority of buy-sell agreements.*

When Is the Ideal Time to Sell Your Business?

Many business owners think, from time to time, about the ideal time to sell their businesses. At the very least, we all think about selling our businesses. The ideal time to sell a business – or your interest in a business – can be described as follows:

- ⊚ **When the business is ready for sale.** Sales are rising, profits are improving, capable management is in place, the balance sheet is reasonably financed and in good position, and growth is on the horizon.

- ⊚ **When the stock market is rising and the outlook is favorable.** Relatively high stock prices encourage relatively high transaction prices.

- ⊚ **When the industry is hot.** It is apparent that a rising tide lift all boats. A good transaction for your company is more likely to happen when good transactions are happening with companies like yours.

- ⊚ **When low-cost financing is available.** Better pricing occurs when cheap financing is available on reasonable terms.

- ⊚ **When irrational buyers abound.** You never want to be an irrational buyer, of course, but if you are selling, it is always good to have irrational, or even strongly motivated, buyers around.

- ⊚ **When the shareholders are ready to sell.** Shareholder readiness can relate to personal estate planning, personal objectives, management succession, and a host of other factors.

To recall a line from the 1969 hit by the Fifth Dimension, "When the moon is in the seventh house and Jupiter aligns with Mars."

When Is the Ideal Time to Trigger Your Buy-Sell Agreement?

You are probably asking, "What in the world does the 'ideal time to sell a business' have to do with buy-sell agreements?" That is a great question.

The answer lies in inter-relatedness. We know intuitively that the best time to sell a business is when all the above factors are in alignment. The fact is that they are quite often not lined up in ideal fashion. If we think about it, we know that the operation of buy-sell agreements occurs inside and alongside business-related cycles.

Since all the factors relating to the ideal time to sell a business are not likely to be in alignment all the time, the inevitable conclusion is that the ideal time to be getting your business and yourself into the best possible position to sell is *all the time.*

Let's look at the potential timing of transactions associated with your buy-sell agreement.

- ◉ As long as you own a business or a significant interest in one, the corporate, industry, market, and financing cycles noted above will be in operation.

- ◉ Superimpose on those cycles the additional uncertainties pertaining to future events for your shareholders. No one knows when anyone will die. But we all know we all will die one day. We just don't know when, or who, will be first.

- ◉ No one knows if or when they will become disabled. At any age, however, the odds of becoming disabled are far higher than those of dying. According to insurance statistics, one in seven Americans will suffer a long-term disability before the age of 65.

- You probably don't know the status of personal estate planning of all your other shareholders. All you know is you are, in all likelihood, procrastinating in taking care of one or more important planning issues.

- When you signed your buy-sell agreement, you weren't so cross-wise with another shareholder that you would want to have them fired. Chances are, that may not be true today. But those situations arise with surprising frequency.

All the factors relating to when a buy-sell agreement will be triggered are not known all the time. Therefore, the ideal time to ensure that your agreement will operate reasonably and leave you, the other shareholders, and the business in reasonable condition is *all the time*.

The underlying purpose of this book is to help you to reduce or eliminate the uncertainties associated with the future operation of your buy-sell agreement.

I'm not a lawyer, so I don't have any legal opinions. However, I do have a number of opinions, and I hope they are not illegal! I am writing from business and business valuation perspectives throughout this book. Once you decide what you want to do from a business point of view, you can get your attorney to help fix your buy-sell agreement. If he or she is a trusted advisor, then get their assistance in working through the business issues first.

The focus of our discussion of buy-sell agreements is on *business owners*. That term is normally used to refer to controlling owners. But every owner – controlling, noncontrolling, or minority – is affected by the operation of buy-sell agreements. So when I refer to business owners here, I am talking about *all business owners*, regardless of the stakes they have in their businesses.

BUY-SELL AGREEMENT – BET AND LOST

A friend of mine told me the following true story. His father was an initial minority shareholder and employee of a business during the early 1960s. At the outset of the enterprise, the shareholders implemented a buy-sell agreement with a fixed price. The father's shares were valued at his investment value of $250,000.

Fast forward to 1974. The business grew and was successful. My friend, who is quite knowledgeable about business valuation, said his father's interest would have been worth more than $1 million by 1974 – the year his father died.

Neither the corporation nor the other shareholders offered to update the price in the buy-sell agreement to purchase the shares from the father's estate, so the shares were purchased for $250,000. My friend noted that receiving $250,000 in 1974, and not $1 million or more, made a significant difference in his mother's independence for the remaining 25 years of her life. In addition, it caused a great deal of bitterness towards his father's former partners.

My friend's father probably did not think in terms of making a bet on his company's buy-sell agreement, but the fact it was not updated created a betting situation. He bet, and his family lost.

> **My challenge to you, your family members, and other owners is to avoid making a bet on your buy-sell agreement.**

CHAPTER THREE

BUSINESS ISSUES & LATENT PROBLEMS

Pete:	**"How long has it been since you put your buy-sell agreement in place?"**

Sam:	"Looks like we signed it almost 14 years ago."

Pete:	**"Has anyone reviewed the agreement since then?"**

Sam:	"You mean, like by our lawyer, or just internally?"

Pete:	**"Either or both."**

Sam:	"Well, I suppose that William and Don read it when they became shareholders, about 10 years ago. I don't think our attorney has read it. I know I haven't asked him to look at it, and I don't think George has either."

Pete:	**"Is your company a party to contracts or agreements with other businesses?"**

Sam:	"Quite a few. We have several important supplier relationships that are contractual in nature. And, we have contracts with our largest two customers."

Pete:	**"Do you or your attorney review these when they are signed?"**

Sam:	"Of course we do! It would be irresponsible not to!"

Pete:	**"Do these contracts get adjusted or amended over time?"**

Sam:	"Sure. We have to keep them current in order to be sure that our key business relationships will run smoothly. When things change, the contracts have to be changed accordingly."

Pete:	**"And how long has it been since your buy-sell agreement was reviewed?"**

Sam:	"OK, OK. I see what you are talking about."

Key Business Issues

Buy-sell agreements are legal contracts. What is not clearly understood, however, is that they are also business and valuation documents. We refer to buy-sell agreements this way because they represent contractual agreements between the respective parties concerning the following:

- **Business objectives.** Buy-sell agreements are designed to facilitate business objectives of companies and their shareholders including:

    - Limiting ownership to an existing group or family (or multiple families).

    - Maintaining relative ownership between or among groups of shareholders.

    - Integrating the operation of a buy-sell agreement with the estate planning of one or more owners.

    - Limiting the ability of parties to the agreement to sell their shares, except pursuant to the terms of the agreement.

- ◉ **Pricing.** Buy-sell agreements determine how the pricing of transactions will be determined. In other words, buy-sell agreements determine how the *valuation* of businesses (or business ownership interests) will be determined in future transactions that may or will occur.

- ◉ **Terms.** Buy-sell agreements also dictate the terms upon which future transactions will occur.

Let me reiterate. This book is written from the perspective of a businessman and a business valuation expert. It is based on personal experiences spanning more than 30 years. I have reviewed hundreds of buy-sell agreements and been involved in dozens of what, for lack of a better term, I'll call "buy-sell agreements gone bad."

These experiences suggest that the *vast majority* of existing agreements contain (or omit) language that will almost certainly create the potential for problems when they are triggered. *As I have said previously, and will continue to reiterate, your buy-sell agreement likely has these same problems.*

Some buy-sell agreements will accomplish their objectives. However, buy-sell agreements often offer proof of the law of unintended consequences – most do not and will not facilitate desired or desirable results. The *main problem* is companies and their shareholders simply do not know what could or might happen when their agreements are triggered. Doesn't that word itself suggest potential problems or at least a crisis of some sort?

The majority of agreements we have seen in operation have not worked anything like the parties anticipated or desired when their terms were invoked. We will examine a number of examples throughout the book. Our objective is to learn from experience and to anticipate potential problems.

Latent Problems with Buy-Sell Agreements

There are many reasons for latent problems in buy-sell agreements. We have alluded to several of these thus far.

Potential problems include:

- **Agreements are dated.** The buy-sell agreements in many companies date back to their inception. If your company was formed in the 1970s or 1980s or 1990s or early 2000s, your agreement may well be dated. Often, when agreements are updated, they are not reviewed from business and valuation perspectives.

- **Valuation language is dated.** The vocabulary of business appraisal has evolved over the last 30 years. There is a better understanding today among business appraisers of the conceptual meaning of different "types" or "levels" of value.

- **Valuation language is imprecise.** Too often, the language used to describe the pricing mechanism or valuation process is imprecise. While this result is unintended, attorneys and owners are generally not familiar with valuation vocabulary and concepts, but the language in your agreement will be binding on all parties when it is triggered.

- **Failure to focus.** Chances are the owners never did focus clearly on their business intentions when their agreements were created.

- **Overlooking important elements.** Life insurance, for example, is quite often used as a funding mechanism for the operation of buy-sell agreements upon the death of an owner. Too often, the interaction between buy-sell agreements and life insurance is overlooked or not precisely defined. There are many other business elements that are often not considered.

- **Changing business and personal objectives.** Corporate needs change, as do the personal desires and objectives of individual shareholders. Over time, it seems to become increasingly difficult for owners with diverging or divergent interests to talk about their buy-sell agreements. For example, few of us like to talk about dying, so it is easy to procrastinate.

It is one thing to identify a problem. It is quite another to attempt to fix it. Solving issues with your buy-sell agreement will require outside help. This book does not replace the need for competent legal counsel. If anything, we strongly urge you to listen more carefully to your attorney when agreements are prepared or revised. Our intent is to assist lawyers, other professional advisors to corporations, and owners in accomplishing their desired business objectives. Consider purchasing copies of this book for your key advisors. It will help them better help you.

You Will Be a Buyer or a Seller

Consider the following general definition of a buy-sell agreement from my perspective as a businessman:

- Buy-sell agreements are contracts by and among the shareholders (or equity partners of a legal entity) of a business and, with corporate agreements, the business itself.

- They establish the mechanism for the purchase of equity interests following the death (or other adverse or significant changes) of one of the owners.

- In the case of corporate joint ventures, they also establish the value for break-ups or for circumstances calling for one corporate venture partner to buy out the other partner.

Buy-sell agreements are important because they represent agreement between a corporation and its shareholders regarding how *future* transactions contemplated by the agreements will occur.

At the time most buy-sell agreements are initiated, either the interests of the corporation and the shareholders are aligned, or they are not sufficiently misaligned to prevent agreement from taking place. But such agreement often does not occur.

Perhaps the apparent alignment of interests lulls owners into complacency. In most cases, corporate counsel tries, often mightily, to have shareholders focus on their buy-sell agreements. Nevertheless, despite their best efforts, the shareholders often do not listen.

- They do not want to spend the time or mental energy.
- They do not want to spend the money.
- They just want to get on with their lives.

The fact is, prior to the initiation of a buy-sell agreement, it seems that few owners take sufficient time to understand the exact nature of their agreements, how they will work in the future, and the implications for them.

If you don't know whether you will be a seller or a buyer (or perhaps both over time) under your buy-sell agreement, isn't it a good idea to do your best to ensure that it will work for you (and the other shareholders), whether you end up being buyers or sellers?

It is important to talk about the future when the interests of the parties are aligned, or at least not sufficiently misaligned to prevent discussion. Know this for certain: When your buy-sell agreement is triggered, the interests of the parties will diverge.

SOMETHING TO PONDER

The other guy will not always be the first to die or to leave the company. It might be you. However, your buy-sell agreement is indifferent to timing. It will apply to you (and the other owners) whether you will be buyers or sellers.

- If you know you will be a buyer, you would always prefer to buy at the lowest possible price.

- If you know you will be a seller, you would prefer to sell at the highest possible price.

- If you don't know which you will be and you act rationally, you will likely desire pricing in the buy-sell agreement that is reasonable regardless of future outcomes.

Rational conversations with all the shareholders to key aspects of your buy-sell agreement will lead to workable agreements. These conversations are sometimes difficult. My challenge to you is to have them anyway.

Chapter Four

Business Factors to Consider

Pete:	**"Sam, how is your company organized?"**
Sam:	"What do you mean?"
Pete:	**"I know you are incorporated, but are you a C corporation or an S corporation?"**
Sam:	"We are an S corporation now, but we used to be a C corporation."
Pete:	**"When did you change?"**
Sam:	"Well, when we brought William and Don on board about 10 years ago, our accountant suggested that we make an S corporation election. He said that with our growing success and new owners, it would be difficult to bonus out all the earnings and it would be better to make distributions."
Pete:	**"Did you make any changes to the buy-sell agreement after you changed corporate forms?"**
Sam:	"Pete, you know the answer already. We haven't changed the a single thing since we signed it 14 years ago."

An Estate Planner's Guide to Buy-Sell Agreements for the Closely Held Business, by Louis A. Mezzullo, provides a list of factors to consider when creating buy-sell agreements.[1] The list of factors in the following discussion borrows from Mr. Mezzullo's book. However, unless otherwise indicated, the comments are mine based on my experience.

1. **Nature of the entity.** There are a variety of organizational forms that have different considerations for buy-sell agreement purposes.

    - **C corporations.** C corporations are taxable entities and must pay their own state and federal income taxes.

    - **S corporations.** S corporations must restrict ownership to appropriate types and numbers of shareholders. An S corporation buy-sell agreement should be designed to preserve the election by preventing the number of shareholders to increase above the legal maximum and also preventing ineligible shareholders from holding stock.

    - **Professional corporation.** It may be necessary to limit ownership of certain professional corporations to shareholders with particular licenses or credentials. A CPA firm, for example, might want to limit ownership to individuals holding the CPA certificate. An insurance brokerage firm might decide to limit ownership to individuals holding certain licenses.

---

1   Mezzullo, Louis A., *An Estate Planner's Guide to Buy-Sell Agreements for the Closely Held Business, Second Edition,* (American Bar Association, 2007), pp. 11-14.

- **Tax pass-through entities.** S corporations, limited partnerships, and limited liability companies may need to implement provisions to ensure distributions are at least sufficient for owners to pay personal income taxes associated with entity earnings.

2. **Size of the entity.** Often, complexity in ownership develops as companies increase in size and value. While companies are small, remaining shareholders may agree to purchase the shares of departing shareholders in cross-purchase agreements, often funded by life insurance (in the event of death). As the number of owners and value increases, such agreements become cumbersome or unworkable. In addition, life insurance will not work to fund the purchase of shares of an owner who was terminated. Interesting issues can arise when corporations continue to hold life insurance policies on the lives of owners who leave for reasons other than death.

3. **Valuation of the entity/interest.** Addressing the valuation question is a primary focus of this book. Whether the company is buying or you are selling, the price at which a buy-sell transaction occurs is important for both – and the remaining shareholders as well.

   - Quite often, the interest being sold pursuant to buy-sell agreements is the largest single asset of the selling shareholder. Achieving a reasonable valuation for that interest is of paramount concern.

   - Valuation is also important for the company, which must pay for stock purchases. The remaining owners will benefit from reasonable purchases while their remaining interests will be diluted by unreasonable ones.

- The valuation question is difficult, at best, and warrants focused decision-making in the process of creating or revising a buy-sell agreement.

4. **Relative ownership.** If a company has a dominant shareholder and one or more owners with relatively small interests, the operation of a buy-sell agreement can place hardships on the minority owners who may be required to purchase the shares of the majority shareholder. In such cases, it is helpful to have a corporate buy-sell agreement in place that is funded, hopefully, by life insurance.

   - Alternatively, there may be no controlling shareholder, but the operation of the buy-sell agreement could convey control of the company to one or two shareholders. This may or may not be a desirable outcome and is one that should be considered. An example is illustrative. Assume six owners hold interests of 40, 25, 10, 10, 10, and 5 shares, respectively, of a total of 100 shares. No one controls the company. Now assume that the owner of the 25 shares dies and his shares are repurchased by the company. The 40-share owner now owns 40 shares out of a total of 75 shares, or 53.3% of the stock. Control has shifted, perhaps as an unintended or unanticipated function of the operation of the buy-sell agreement.

   - If there are multiple families or groups of owners, it may be desirable to provide that the operation of the buy-sell agreement maintains the original relative ownership positions between them.

   - In some companies, shareholders may be given the right to purchase a departing owner's shares on a pro rata basis in order to maintain relative ownership percentages. Occasionally, companies are owned by "groups" of shareholders, for example, by the descendants of two families. The buy-sell agreement may be structured to maintain the relative ownership of the two groups, with individual shareholders within the groups making the necessary decisions to maintain their relative ownership positions.

5. **Ages of the owners.** While even young owners can die or have change-of-life experiences, the issue of aging needs to be considered when structuring buy-sell agreements. This is true for the estate planning issues mentioned previously. It is also true for owners nearing normal retirement age.

    •   Buy-sell agreements can provide for a structured purchase of a retiring owner's interest. They may include life insurance to purchase shares in the event of an owner's unexpected death.

    •   If life insurance is not available, or its cost is prohibitive, it may be necessary to provide for a purchase of the departing owner's shares over time.

    •   It is far better to agree on or anticipate these issues before adverse circumstances force their consideration.

6. **Relative financial positions of owners.** Some corporations are financed by highly affluent individuals or other companies. Others are financed by private equity groups or other institutions. Companies financed by sources like these often have managers with ownership interests in the business. Buy-sell agreements may need to consider the relative inequality of wealth of the various owners. Neither

owners nor the corporation should be placed in the position of engaging in transactions they are not financially capable of handling.

7. **Health and insurability of owners.** In the event of the ill health of an owner, it is essential to establish agreement as to how the transition of ownership will occur. For example, what will happen if the shareholder is unable to continue working or in the event of death? If a shareholder is not insurable for health reasons, this factor will need to be addressed in the buy-sell agreement because funding options may be limited.

8. **Commitment of owners to the business and importance of their participation in the business.** Over time, companies often develop groups of "inside" shareholders who are active in a business and other shareholders who are passive owners.

   - It may be appropriate when structuring a buy-sell agreement to provide for the ability of "inside" shareholders to benefit disproportionately from the purchase of a passive owner's shares.

   - Rights of first refusal are common in such circumstances, because "inside" shareholders want to ensure that new passive owners are acceptable to them. See Chapter 12 for more detailed discussion of rights of first refusal.

9. **Availability of assets for redeeming the interest.** It is important to consider the financing of future stock purchases.

   - If life insurance is to be used, it is critical to coordinate the use of proceeds directly with the buy-sell agreement. Considerably more on this issue is found in Chapters 13 and 15.

- If a sinking fund is developed, agreement should be reached over the consideration of sinking fund assets in the valuation. After all, sinking fund assets are developed while all shareholders are here and are used to redeem a departing shareholder(s).

- If it is anticipated that there will be insufficient assets for a company to redeem an interest, or if life insurance is not available, then it may be appropriate for the shareholders to have cross-purchase agreements in place to handle transfers outside the corporation. This could be problematic in the event one or more shareholders lack the financial capacity to make such a purchase, which may become impracticable as the number of shareholders grows beyond a small number.

10. **State law with respect to stock redemptions in the case of a corporation or distributions to members of an LLC.** Mezzullo cites certain Virginia statutes and notes that drafters of buy-sell agreements must be concerned that their operation will not render a corporation insolvent. He states:

> Most states prohibit a corporation or LLC from making a redemptive distribution to a shareholder or member if doing so will leave it unable to pay its debts when due in the usual course of business, or if as a result its assets will become less than the total of its liabilities plus any amounts needed to satisfy any preferential distribution rights held by shareholders or members that are superior to those of the distributee if the corporation or LLC were to be then dissolved.[2]

---

2   Ibid, p. 13.

11. **Existence of restrictions under loan agreements.** Lenders often place restrictions on a company's ability to utilize corporate assets to repurchase shares if doing so would diminish creditworthiness below threshold levels. These matters are often negotiated in the context of loan agreements, and the impact of such covenants should be considered in the structure of buy-sell agreements.

12. **Family relationships among the owners.** Family relationships can influence the tax treatment of proceeds from the sale of stock pursuant to buy-sell agreements. Such relationships can also create special needs for transferring ownership within the family (or families, when more than one family is involved in ownership).

   • Family tax issues are beyond the scope of this book. As Mezullo points out, family relationships may have an impact regarding applicability of special valuation rules in the Internal Revenue Code's Chapter 23. Please consult your estate planning attorney if this comment is applicable to you.

   • If members of a single family own all or substantially all of the shares of a business, the buy-sell agreement may need to address intra-family transfers. For example, if two brothers started a business and they now have children in the business, the agreement may need to allow for each brother to gift or otherwise transfer shares to his children. The transferred shares would then be subject to the terms of the agreement.

   • When more than one family is involved in ownership, the agreement may need to address how overall family ownership is maintained. The agreement may need to address how relative ownership between the two families will be treated such that there is not, for example, an unexpected change of control through the operation of the buy-sell agreement.

13. **Working relationships among the owners.** In an ideal world, all working owners would get along wonderfully. The world is rarely ideal, and some owners do not get along well with others as the strains of running a business and life tear at their loyalties. Even if all owners are getting along when an agreement is signed, there is always potential for disagreement. Despite the difficulties in addressing issues of conflict or potential conflict, your buy-sell agreement may need to address such relationships, particularly regarding management deadlocks. These are not easy issues, and they do not become any easier *after* a deadlock has been reached!

14. **Licensing/qualification requirements.** Some professions require licensure to practice. If your company is a law firm or an engineering firm, for example, it may be appropriate or even required to restrict ownership to those who are licensed attorneys or engineers.

Mezullo also raises the issue of potential conflicts when the company or shareholders have legal representation. It is fairly common for a company's counsel to participate in the drafting of its buy-sell agreement. In the process, he or she may give advice to the controlling shareholder that is not provided to other owners. It is often a good idea for individual owners to obtain independent legal representation to review their agreements from their own perspectives. A company's counsel will most often advise individual owners to seek the advice of independent counsel. In fact, in some cases, you may be asked to acknowledge you have either sought independent legal advice or were offered the opportunity to do so and did not. It may be appropriate for the company to pay for independent counsel for the other shareholders.

It is clear there are a number of important factors to be taken into account when preparing a buy-sell agreement, some of which will be of relatively more importance to particular shareholders. Most of these factors (and many more) are included in the *Buy-Sell Agreement Audit Checklist* (found at www.buysellagreementsonline.com) for your consideration.

PRENUPTIAL AGREEMENTS AND BUY-SELL AGREEMENTS

Prenuptial agreements (or "prenups") may be unromantic, but they may make good sense.

Prenups are the result of conversations between couples regarding what happens to whose assets and income in the event that the couple divorces. They are increasingly being used when couples marry, particularly for the second (or third, or more) time.

> "More and more, these agreements are being drafted. It's not just for the rich and famous any longer. It's for people that have assets and/or income that they want to protect." *Marlene Eskind Moses, President of the American Academy of Matrimonial Lawyers.*

Buy-sell agreements are supposed to be the result of conversations among owners of businesses addressing what will happen when lots of trigger events – including divorce – occur. The objectives of such agreements are to protect the interests of the company and the individual shareholders consistent with mutual fairness. Sometimes, however, the owners may not talk – or pay attention when others are talking – about important provisions.

I read a buy-sell agreement that addressed the divorce of owners. It provided that in the event any owner became divorced, the company had the right to repurchase 100% of his shares. Period. That's it. Normally, divorce provisions in buy-sell agreements are there to prevent shares owned by a divorcing spouse from being split by divorce courts and awarded to non-owner employee spouses.

Suppose an owner of this company had a prenup agreement protecting his ownership interest from division in divorce. Wouldn't he be surprised when his fellow owners enforced the agreement and purchased his shares? Suppose he did not have a prenup and arranged things in the divorce to protect his interest in the company? He'd still be surprised if the agreement was enforced.

I'm not saying this will happen, but it could.

My challenge to you is to be sure you know what your buy-sell agreement says in the event an owner is divorced. How would the provisions apply if another owner (not you) got divorced? How about you? Are any prenup agreements coordinated with the operation of the buy-sell agreement? These are good questions to consider.

CHAPTER FIVE

THE MOVING PARTS OF BUY-SELL AGREEMENTS

Pete:	**"Sam, when you put your buy-sell agreement together 14 years ago, how much time did you spend on it?"**
Sam:	"Well, as I recall, George and I met with our attorney for a couple of hours and we talked about a few things. Then, we got a draft of the agreement back. George and I were going to meet to go over it, but that never happened. I guess I spent about half an hour reading it over before I signed it."
Pete:	**"And how about George?"**
Sam:	"I think it is safe to say he never read it at all. He just hates to read any of the legal stuff and leaves that to the rest of us."
Pete:	**"What about William and Don?"**
Sam:	"When they came on board as owners, I told them to look over the buy-sell agreement because it was important they sign on as parties to it. Our attorney told me to be sure I told him when we were taking on a couple of new shareholders. I told them to ask our attorney if they had any questions."
Pete:	**"Did they talk to the attorney?"**
Sam:	"No, I don't think so. But they signed it."

Key Aspects of Buy-Sell Agreements

From valuation and business perspectives, buy-sell agreements generally incorporate several important aspects defining their operation. Specifically, buy-sell agreements that have reasonable prospects for working successfully:

1. **Require agreement** *at a point in time* among shareholders of a company and/or between shareholders and the company.

2. **Relate to transactions** that may or will occur *at future points in time* between the shareholders, or between the shareholders and the corporation.

3. **Define the conditions** that will cause the buy-sell provisions to be triggered. Most often, business owners think of death as the most likely trigger event for buy-sell agreements. It is actually the least likely event to happen for most companies.

4. **Determine the price** at which the identified future transactions will occur (as in price per share, per unit, or per member interest). This is one of the hardest parts of establishing effective buy-sell agreements.

5. **Determine the terms** under which the price will be paid.

6. **Provide for funding** so the contemplated transactions can occur on terms and conditions satisfactory to selling owners and the corporation (or other purchasing owners). This element is important and often overlooked.

7. **Satisfy the business requirements of the parties.** While buy-sell agreements have much in common, each business situation is different, and unique parties are involved. In the end, legal counsel must draft buy-sell agreements to address the business issues that are important to the parties. Clearly, establishing and agreeing on the key business issues and having them reflected in the

agreement can be difficult. Know this for certain: If you and the other owners do not reach agreement on key business issues, *no attorney* can draft a reasonable document for you.

8. **Provide support for estate tax planning** for the shareholders, whether in family companies or in non-family situations. The Internal Revenue Service has rules to determine whether the price determined in a buy-sell agreement – even if binding on the parties – is also determinative of fair market value for estate tax purposes. Recent court cases have also addressed the issue. If a buy-sell agreement is expected to be used as an estate planning tool, it is essential that tax advisors work with legal counsel and valuation advisors to ensure the agreement will meet both business and estate planning objectives.

9. **Satisfy legal requirements** relating to the operation of the agreements. Buy-sell agreements must be drafted such that they are legally binding on the parties to them. In addition, agreements must be drafted to comply with laws and/or regulations that may be applicable to their operation. Business owners must rely on legal counsel regarding such matters.

Buy-Sell Agreements Are Common to All Industries and Corporate Forms

Many business owners think their industry is different than all other industries in its unique problems and issues. Within their industry, they assume, their company is also unique. They are partially right.

Buy-sell agreements, however, are used in every industry where different owners have potentially divergent desires and needs – and that includes every industry we have seen to date.

The focus of the book is on companies in any industry with four primary characteristics:

- **Substantial value.** There are many hundreds of thousands of businesses that might be categorized as "mom and pop" enterprises (with no disrespect whatsoever), and generally do not attain significant economic value. We will focus on businesses of substantial value, or those with millions of dollars of value (as low as $2 or $3 million) and ranging upwards to many billions in value. Nevertheless, much of the information in this book is relevant to businesses of virtually any size.

- **Privately owned.** When there is an active public market for a company's securities, there is generally no need for buy-sell agreements. Note that this definition also applies to joint ventures involving one or more publicly traded companies where the joint ventures themselves are not publicly traded.

- **Multiple shareholders.** Most businesses of substantial economic value have two or more shareholders. The number of shareholders may range from a small number of founders or initial investors to many dozens, or even hundreds, of shareholders in multi-generational and/or multi-family enterprises.

- **Corporate buy-sell agreements.** Many smaller companies, and even some of significant size, have cross-purchase buy-sell agreements. While much of the book will be helpful for companies with such agreements, the focus here is on companies that have corporate agreements. In other words, the buy-sell agreement includes the company as a party to the agreement, along with the shareholders.

If your business has substantial economic value and you have multiple shareholders, this book is written for you. The "you" in the previous sentence pertains regardless of whether you are the controlling shareholder, the CEO, the CFO, the general counsel, a director, a working manager-employee, or a nonworking (in the business) investor.

The content of this book is applicable regardless of the corporate form of organization for your business. Buy-sell agreements are necessary and/or appropriate for all corporate forms, including:

- Corporations, whether organized as S corporations or as C corporations

- Limited liability companies

- Partnerships, whether between individuals or between entities, such as corporate joint ventures

- Not-for-profit organizations, particularly those with for-profit activities

- Joint ventures between organizations (quite often overlooked)

This is *not* a book on how to draft buy-sell agreements. We'll address such issues elsewhere with benefit of counsel. It is a book calling for appropriate utilization of business and valuation expertise in the process of examining existing or new buy-sell agreements. As can be seen in the discussion just above, its applicability spreads to all corporate forms and to portions of agreements, like joint venture agreements, which provide for similar buy-sell provisions.

The Buy-Sell Agreement Checkup

It takes time, effort, thought, and resources to create and maintain workable buy-sell agreements. However, there is a problem with buy-sell agreements that may be understood through the following analogy:

⊚   When we get a fever, we typically take aspirin and rest. If the fever persists, most of us will go to a doctor to find out the source of the fever and address whatever symptoms exist. If we have heart disease and don't know it and there are no external symptoms, the first sign of a problem may be a heart attack. At that point, you do whatever you can, but sometimes it is too late.

⊚   Most people I know after the age of 50 or so have regular checkups, including EKGs and other tests that physicians consider appropriate. One of the purposes of these checkups is to identify problems early so they can be treated or avoided.

There is no fever with your buy-sell agreement to warn you of potential problems. Keep in mind that there are there are very few planned checkups for such agreements. Consider reading this book as the first of a series of regular buy-sell agreement checkups. Discover any problems now so the agreement can be changed to avoid the catastrophic problem that may be lurking in the words on the pages.

Mock Trigger Events

Let me ask, as you proceed with your reading, that you keep this question in mind: "What will happen if there is a trigger event, like the death of one of our owners, and our buy-sell agreement is put into operation?"   I encourage you to consider a series of mock trigger events from a variety of perspectives.   Think through the implications.   Outline the process. Talk about it with your other owners and advisors.   Your objective is to know that your agreement will work without triggering it.

The Buy-Sell Agreement Audit Checklist

To assist in that process, and in the process of considering mock trigger events, we have developed the *Buy-Sell Agreement Audit Checklist*. This checklist is available free to readers of this book. It is available in PDF format to facilitate your use. Download it and share it with your fellow owners and advisors. Go to www.buysellagreementsonline.com. Order the checklist, which retails for $19.95, and enter the discount code "FREE" to receive your free copy.

PROTECTING YOUR MOST IMPORTANT ASSET

Step aside from your role as a corporate officer or director for a moment. What portion of your personal net worth is tied up in your ownership of your privately held company? If you are like many private business owners, the percentage is significant, surprising, or even scary.

Your buy-sell agreement has, or should have, a number of "moving parts." Lots of conflicting interests must be satisfied or at least reasonably resolved. If you think you can find the solution for your particular situation in a book of "forms" on the Internet (or in your attorney's office or computer), then think again.

Please complete the following right now. Do not go looking for information. Make even the grossest of estimates and perform the indicated calculations. This is only an "order of magnitude" calculation. Make the best guesses you can right now:

1. Value of your interest in your closely held business?
   [$_____]

2. Value of all other investment assets, including home(s)?
   [$_____]

3. Add #1 and #2 together.
    [$_____]

4. Total of your interest-bearing debt, including mortgages?
    [$_____]

5. Subtract #4 from #3 (Your "net worth" for this purpose).
    [$_____]

6. Divide #1 (value of your business) into #5 (net worth).
    [_____%]

This percentage is the portion of your net worth accounted for by the illiquid value of your closely held business or interest in one. If you are like many other business owners, this percentage likely exceeds 50% and could be much higher.

My challenge to you is to use this process to protect what is likely your most valuable asset through your buy-sell agreement. You will need the cooperation of your fellow shareholders and assistance from trusted advisors. For further information on this critical issue, see my book, *The One Percent Solution: An Introduction for Wealth Managers and Business Owners to Managing Pre-Liquid Wealth* (available at www.buysellagreementsonline.com).

PART II

BUY-SELL AGREEMENT ESSENTIALS

Chapter Six

Trigger Events: Those Things That Happen

Pete:	**"Sam, do you know what events will trigger your buy-sell agreement?"**
Sam:	"Well, if one of the shareholders dies, the company has to buy his stock. So I guess that is what you call a 'trigger event.' I think the agreement says something about what happens if one of us retires or becomes disabled, but I can't remember the particulars."
Pete:	**"What does the agreement say if one of the owners gets divorced?"**
Sam:	"I think there's something in there, but I can't remember what it says."
Pete:	**"What if the actual language in your agreement came from some form?"**
Sam:	"Now that's a scary thought!"

Overview of Trigger Events

Most of the events that trigger buy-sell agreements are not pleasant to consider, particularly to a group of shareholders who may have just come together for a common business purpose.

Why are such incidents called trigger events? Circumstances could be such that the shareholder most affected by a trigger event has a proverbial gun to his or her head! In the alternative, the company may perceive that it has a gun to its head in order to fulfill the repurchase requirements of a buy-sell agreement.

Buy-sell agreements are designed to accomplish one or more business objectives from one or more of several viewpoints: the corporation, the employee-shareholder, the shareholder who is not an employee, and any remaining shareholders. The buy-sell agreement provides for what happens to the shares of owners who leave, for whatever reason, whether favorable or unfavorable.

From the corporation's viewpoint, the buy-sell agreement may prevent the departing shareholder from retaining his shares.

- By requiring a departing shareholder to sell his or her shares to the corporation, the corporation and remaining shareholders eliminate any potential for conflict over future corporate policies with the departed shareholder.

- The agreement may eliminate the potential for the departed shareholder to benefit from future success of the business created by the remaining shareholders.

- The agreement may also prevent a shareholder (or his or her estate) from selling shares to "undesirable" parties, enabling the remaining shareholders to decide who the next shareholder will be, if any.

These reasons for buy-sell provisions apply to virtually all trigger events.

An Acronym: QFRDDD

The term "trigger" can have a benign connotation. If A happens, then B is triggered or set in motion to happen. However, the majority of trigger events related to buy-sell agreements have less benign connotations.

We use QFRDDD as an acronym to denote the following common trigger events for any party in a buy-sell agreement:

- Quits
- Is Fired
- Retires
- Becomes Disabled
- Dies
- Becomes Divorced

While it is easy to think of these events in personal terms, analogous situations also happen to companies. "Quits" equates to withdrawal from a venture, "disabled" could mean inability to answer a capital call, and "dies" represents bankruptcy of a participant.

Think of QFRDDD to remember:

- **Q – Quits.** A buy-sell agreement may provide a mechanism for shareholders who leave a business to sell their shares to the corporation or other shareholders. A shareholder may quit under a variety of scenarios, some of which are more favorable to the corporation and other shareholders. The circumstances of quitting may determine how the departing shareholder is treated under the buy-sell agreement.

  - **Favorable circumstances.** A shareholder may decide to leave a company to pursue other interests that are not competitive with the activities of the company. Assuming the ability to fund the purchase, the company and remaining shareholders are likely to view such a departure on favorable terms.

- **Unfavorable circumstances.** Alternatively, a shareholder may decide to leave a company and to pursue competitive activities. Under such circumstances, the company and remaining shareholders may be reluctant to pay full price (whatever that means – to be determined as we proceed) and desire to stretch out payment as long as possible. After all, no one wants to finance a competitor!

⊚ **F – Fired.** When an employee-shareholder is terminated, most corporations desire to retain control over the shares.

- Terminations generally result in diverse, or more likely, adverse interests between the fired shareholder, the corporation, and remaining shareholders.

  - From the employee's viewpoint, the buy-sell agreement assures that his or her shares can be sold at the buy-sell price and creates a market for the shares.

  - From the corporation's viewpoint, buy-sell agreements create the right or the obligation to purchase the departing shareholder's shares.

- A repurchase requirement on termination also eliminates the potential for the terminated shareholder to benefit from any future success of the business created by the remaining employees and shareholders.

- Some agreements call for a penalty to the valuation in cases of termination, particularly for cause. It is important that the parties exercise care regarding potential valuation penalties and that their agreements be explicit regarding when and/or how such penalties would be applied.

⊚ **R – Retires.** The retirement of an employee-shareholder creates a potential divergence of interests between the shareholder and the corporation.

- The shareholder may desire current liquidity over the uncertain future performance of the corporation.

- The corporation may desire not to have potential interference or disagreement with corporate policy, or to have the retired shareholder benefit from future appreciation in value.

- The corporation and the remaining shareholders likely do not want a retired employee to continue to benefit from their ongoing efforts.

⊚ **D – Disabled.** After a defined period of time, the corporation may have the right (from its viewpoint) or the obligation (perhaps, from the employee's viewpoint) to purchase the disabled employee's shares. If disability is a trigger event, it is essential to have a clear definition of what "disability" means. If the company carries disability insurance for key owners, one simple definition of disability for buy-sell agreements is that of the insurance carrier. If the carrier considers a shareholder to be disabled and begins to make disability payments under the policy, the disability clause of a buy-sell agreement could become effective on the date of first payment.

⊙ **D – Dies.** The death of a shareholder creates issues that are often resolved by buy-sell agreements.

- If a shareholder dies owning a minority or controlling interest in a corporation for which there is no market for its shares, the illiquidity of the stock can create estate tax issues.

  - The shares must be valued for estate tax purposes, and the appraisal amount will add to the estate's value.

  - To the extent that the estate is taxable, there may be no liquidity to pay the estate taxes.

  - Buy-sell agreements provide a mechanism for determining the value of shares that may be applicable for estate tax purposes and for monetizing that value for the estate, generally in cash or in a term note (or a combination of the two).

  - The shareholder's estate realizes liquidity and can pay taxes due. As result, the estate can minimize the combination of uncertainties of independent valuation and the certainty of payment of taxes in the absence of liquidity.

- From the corporation's viewpoint, the buy-sell agreement eliminates the need to address uncertain ownership dictated by the deceased shareholder's will and can create the requirement for funding.

⊙ **D – Divorce.** Unfortunately, divorce is quite common today.

- When any group of investors comes together, one of the most likely things that will happen in their collective futures is that one or more of them will be divorced.

- Because of this, most buy-sell agreements have provisions enabling the corporation (or the other shareholders) to purchase shares that otherwise might be granted to the working (or non-owner) spouse in a property settlement decree in a divorce.

- The purpose of divorce provisions in buy-sell agreements is, of course, to prevent shares from falling into the hands of potentially unfriendly ex-spouses.

While it is true that all of the QFRDDD trigger events are important for buy-sell agreements, there are numerous other events that you may want to consider in your buy-sell agreement or in the agreements of your clients.

The 20 Ds of Buy-Sell Agreements

A number of potential trigger events happen to begin with the letter D. In fact, if you do a Google search using the term "Ds of buy-sell agreements," you will find several references to sources addressing Ds in this context.

As a thought teaser, I decided to list some of the many Ds that could be trigger events or otherwise need to be considered in your buy-sell agreement or related shareholder agreements. If one of these Ds is appropriate for consideration in your buy-sell agreement, make note for future discussion. With only brief comments, the *20 Ds of Buy-Sell Agreements* include:

1. **Departure.** An employee quits and leaves employment. This is identical to the Q for quits above.

2. **Discharge.** An employee may be discharged and the buy-sell agreement is triggered.

3. **Death.** Discussed above.

4. **Divorce.** Discussed above.

5. **Disability.** Discussed above.

6. **Default.** This can be another name for situations involving personal bankruptcy and other involuntary transfers. The corporation and remaining shareholders will want to protect against having a bankrupt owner's shares falling into unfriendly hands in the bankruptcy process.

7. **Disqualification.** This can be an important factor in businesses requiring licensing or regulatory approval. For example, if an owner is rendered disqualified to sell insurance or securities by state regulators, the other shareholders may desire that such disqualification be considered a trigger event for the buy-sell agreement.

8. **Disaffection.** This may seem a stretch, but sometimes owner-employees quit in place and need to be discharged.

9. **Disagreement.** Interestingly, when I ask groups of people what the most common triggers for buy-sell agreements are, they almost always place divorce and disagreement (or deadlock) as first and second. However, many buy-sell agreements do not address the potential issue of disagreement or deadlock. Should yours?

10. **Disclosure.** The shareholders' agreement may need to address the need to maintain confidentiality of competitive information and intellectual property. This is important at all times, of course, but even more so in the event that a shareholder departs, for whatever reason.

11. **Dispute resolution.** The parties to an agreement may want to provide for specific procedures in the event that otherwise irresolvable disputes arise. The parties may agree,

for example, that certain disputes are to be resolved through binding arbitration, as well as the procedures for setting up and paying for the arbitration process.

12. **Dilution.** When corporations sell or issue additional shares, the ownership percentages of existing shareholders may be diluted. The shareholders may want to agree in their buy-sell agreement on procedures to protect against their being diluted by the issuance of new shares. Such provisions would prevent a share issuance without notice and would provide the affirmative opportunity to participate in the issuance pro rata to their ownership.

13. **Dividends.** It may be appropriate to agree on dividend policy, particularly in early or growth stages of a company's life, or when the company has debt outstanding. If agreement is not reached in the formative stages of a business, then dividend policy will be determined by the controlling shareholder or group of shareholders that exercises control.

14. **Distributions.** If the company is an S corporation or other tax pass-through entity, it is a good idea to document an agreement to make distributions to shareholders, at a minimum, for their pro rata share of personal taxes generated by income at the entity level.

15. **Drag-along rights.** A controlling shareholder may desire to have what are called "drag-along" rights. If, for example, she obtains an offer for her shares representing 75% of the stock, she may wish to be able to force (by agreement, of course) the remaining 25% of the shares to sell with her. This might occur when a buyer would purchase not less than 100% of the shares.

- **Tag-along rights.** While not a D, the corollaries to drag-along rights are known as "tag-along" rights. With a tag-along provision, the minority shareholders can force (by agreement, of course) the majority shareholder to arrange for the sale of their shares at the same time and for the same price and terms as the controlling shareholder receives. This would prevent a controlling shareholder from selling only a control block, leaving the remaining shareholders in a minority position with a new and unknown owner.

16. **Double entities.** Many owners of companies desire to separate the ownership of real property from the operating company. The purposes for this separation can be to protect the property legally, to provide a separate entity for estate planning purposes, to isolate financing arrangements, and many others. If there is parallel ownership between operating company and a real estate entity, it may be appropriate to have parallel terms in their respective buy-sell agreements.

17. **Differential pricing.** Sometimes owners agree to differential pricing for purposes of their buy-sell agreements depending upon circumstances of the triggering event (or departure). Assume there is a price for purposes of the agreement determined by appraisal or the "Purchase Price." The following are certainly not recommendations, but are illustrative of what might be agreed to by the owners:

- **Death.** 100% of the Purchase Price.

- **Retirement.** 100% of the Purchase Price.

- **Terminated without cause.** 90% (or 100%) of the Purchase Price.

- **Terminated with cause.** 80% of the Purchase Price.

- **Quit or terminated and competing with company.** 75% of the Purchase Price.

18. **"Don't compete" agreements.** The shareholders may have noncompete agreements in the ordinary course of business. However, the buy-sell agreement could require that a noncompete agreement be signed (reasonable as to length and geography) in the event of a purchase of shares pursuant to the agreement. Noncompete agreements are of sufficient importance to need additional discussion below.

19. **Donate.** The buy-sell agreement may specify under what circumstances stock can be given to spouses, children, charities, etc.

20. **Distributions after a trigger event.** What happens to dividends or distributions during the period of time when a buy-sell agreement is triggered and when the purchase transaction is completed? This question is important when disagreements arise, and many months or years go by before there is resolution.

This list of Ds is not complete, but it is interesting and thought-provoking. There are a number of other situations that might warrant consideration in your buy-sell agreement that don't begin with the letter D. These include:

- **Rights of first refusal.** It is common for buy-sell agreements to contain rights of first refusal to the company, to the other shareholders, or to both. Chapter 12 discusses rights of first refusal in more detail.

- **Optional purchase/sale.** The buy-sell agreement can be optional for the company, the shareholder, or both to buy or to sell. Note than an optional agreement will not specify a completed transaction upon the occurrence of a triggering event.

- **Mandatory purchase/sale.** The agreement calls for mandatory purchase of shares after a triggering event (by the company or the other shareholders at the agreement price and terms) and the mandatory sale by the affected shareholder. Unless a buy-sell agreement is mandatory on both seller and buyer, it does not specify a completed transaction with certainty. Agreements are sometimes made to be optional to ensure "flexibility." This flexibility comes with a high price, both for a company and its shareholders.

- **Life insurance.** If there is corporate life insurance on the lives of owners, the agreement should specify exactly how any proceeds are to be treated in terms of valuation of shares. Chapters 13 and 15 discuss the use of life insurance with buy-sell agreements in detail.

- **Maintenance of S corporation status.** The agreement may prevent any shareholder from taking any action with respect to the shares that would jeopardize the S corporation election.

- **Who owns the stock after a trigger event?** This is a question that is seldom addressed but is of vital importance. The basic question is the following: After a trigger event, does an affected shareholder retain the rights and privileges of ownership (to vote, to receive distributions, to receive financial information, etc.), or are his shares converted into a right to receive the Purchase Price (or whatever term is used) pursuant to the terms of the buy-sell agreement?

- **Control maintenance.** Many companies are owned by individuals or families. Their buy-sell agreements may call for provisions that maintain the relative ownership of the respective families when stock transactions occur.

- **Vote restrictions or agreements.** The owners of a business may agree to vote collectively on certain issues. It could be a provision that upon departure of a shareholder and prior to his shares being purchased, the shares are automatically converted to nonvoting shares.

◉ **Personal guarantees.** Sometimes shareholders who are subject to a buy-sell agreement provide a personal guarantee of corporate debt. They may desire that the corporation and other shareholders agree to take all necessary actions to remove (or to attempt to remove) an owner from the personal guarantee if he or she ceases to be a shareholder.

The listings above are not complete, even in combination. However, it is a good idea to have a reasonably comprehensive list of potential provisions in mind as you read more about buy-sell agreements and begin to think about your own agreement.

It should be clear from the above that buy-sell agreements can be favorable from the viewpoints of employee-shareholders, nonemployee-shareholders, the corporation, and any remaining shareholders in many diverse situations. The emphasis is on "can be" because the operation of a buy-sell agreement can go awry despite the best intentions of its creators.

In conclusion, buy-sell agreements are designed to provide objective means of transferring ownership in controlled and predetermined ways under specified circumstances that may be difficult.

In the absence of a workable buy-sell agreement, the remaining shareholders and the corporation may be placed in the unenviable position of negotiating under adverse circumstances with former friends, their families, or their estates. Such negotiations, which would occur after the interests of the parties have diverged, are difficult, fraught with uncertainty, and often lead to litigation.

Workable buy-sell agreements are the cure for the potential problems discussed above.

Noncompete Agreements

Noncompete agreements can be represented as a separate term in an employment contract or as a separate agreement. Noncompete agreements are sometimes referred to as covenants not to compete. The use of noncompete agreements is usually based on the possibility that an employee can do harm to a company upon departure. For example, upon departure or termination, an employee might be able to work for a competitor using knowledge of a company's proprietary information to competitive advantage.

This knowledge could be in the form of intimate knowledge of the former employer's operations, knowledge of specific trade secrets, relationships developed at the former employer's expense, or knowledge of future plans.

Noncompete agreements are also used by some companies to help them retain employees. Quite simply, it is more difficult to change jobs within a particular industry when an employee has signed a noncompete agreement. On the other hand, noncompete agreements are often difficult to enforce. As a general rule, courts tend to dismiss noncompete agreements that are overly broad in terms of either their length or their geographic coverage.

As I have made clear, I am not a lawyer and not an expert in noncompete agreements. However, such agreements are often tied to the operation of buy-sell agreements. The remaining owners of a company have no desire to capitalize a departing owner through the purchase of his or her shares and then have the departed owner compete with the former enterprise.

The logic of this thinking is quite understandable, particularly if a departing owner is a "key" employee with critical knowledge of operations, sales, customer relationships, plans, production, or any other key aspect of a business. In all likelihood, the valuation mechanism – whether through agreement, formula, or appraisal – will not take into account the potential damage of competition by a former owner/employee. Remaining owners will never desire to pay full price to a departing owner and then have their remaining shares devalued by competition by the former owner.

When preparing or reviewing your buy-sell agreement, counsel will likely recommend that the owners consider having a requirement that departing owners who sell their shares back to the company sign a noncompete agreement prior to departure (or prior to payment for shares). This matter is clearly one that should be a topic of informed discussion by the owners when creating a buy-sell agreement. If the issue is not addressed, it is a topic for discussion when reviewing and revising agreements.

Counsel will need to be involved. The law varies from state to state regarding the enforceability of noncompete agreements.

WHO OWNS THE STOCK AFTER A TRIGGER EVENT?

"Who owns the stock after a trigger event?" is an important question. I was retained as an appraiser in a dispute where a company had terminated a key employee. A buy-sell agreement and a valuation dispute were already underway. Two appraisals had already been performed. The former employee's appraiser reached a conclusion at a controlling interest level. The employer's appraiser rendered a conclusion at the nonmarketable minority level. The conclusions were miles apart.

I was retained by the former employee to review both appraisals and to testify at a binding arbitration on the issue of valuation. After reviewing the two appraisals, I concluded that the employee's expert appraisal 1) was rendered at the appropriate level of value, i.e., control, and, 2) was reasonable in its conclusion.

By the time of the arbitration, the employee had been terminated for nearly two years. While reviewing the buy-sell agreement, I reached the conclusion that the agreement provided that she still owned stock. The agreement was specific in converting the shares of a departed employee to nonvoting shares and in limiting access to certain corporate information.

The agreement was silent regarding distributions, but the corporate charter provided that all shares, voting or nonvoting, were to receive distributions pro rata to ownership. Distributions amounted to 100% of earnings over normal salaries for owner-employees. My conclusion was, of course, reached from my perspective as an appraiser and businessman.

The arbitration panel agreed with my analysis. The former employee was awarded about two years of prior distributions as part of the arbitration settlement. Neither the former employee, her attorneys, the employer, nor its attorneys had identified the dividend issue. Needless to say, the remaining owners were dismayed and my client, the former employee, was overjoyed.

> **Many buy-sell agreements do not treat the continuing rights of ownership (or not) following trigger events in specific terms.**
>
> **My challenge to you is to ensure that the owners agree on this important issue. It won't go away because it's ignored. The ox that gets gored could be yours, a member of your family, or a fellow owner.**

CHAPTER SEVEN

CATEGORIES OF BUY-SELL AGREEMENTS

Pete:	"Sam, there are three basic categories of buy-sell agreements. In cross-purchase agreements, the owners agree to buy the other owners out if something happens. In entity agreements, the company does the buying. And finally, there are hybrids, which can go either way. What category does your agreement fit into?"
Sam:	"Well, when we put in the 'new' buy-sell agreement – you know, the one we did 14 years ago – we decided to have the company do the purchasing if anything happened."
Pete:	"Was there an agreement that was in place before that?"
Sam:	"Yeah. When we first started into business more than 20 years ago, we were a partnership. An insurance guy sold us some policies that either of us could use to buy out the other if someone died."
Pete:	"I didn't know that part of your company's history. Why did you change the agreement?"
Sam:	"When we incorporated we had the company purchase the stock instead of us individually. The accountant said it was usually easier to make insurance payments with company-owned policies. He also said that it would be better if we ever added new shareholders."

There are three general categories of buy-sell agreements that are defined by the relationships between the corporation and the shareholders who are subject to the agreements.

- ◉ **Cross-purchase agreements.** Cross-purchase agreements are agreements between and among the shareholders of a corporation calling for the purchase by the other shareholder(s) of the shares subject to the buy-sell agreement.

  - Cross-purchase agreements are often funded by life insurance owned by shareholder(s) on the lives of other shareholders.

  - Cross-purchase agreements quickly become unworkable as the number of shareholders increases and as market value grows. See Figure 2 for an illustration of the growing complexity of cross purchase agreements.

  - Cross-purchase agreements normally require individual owners to finance stock purchases that are not related to a death. They may or may not have that capability.

  - Cross-purchase agreements are also used in many businesses that are owned by one family. They do so to avoid the potential tax problems inherent in the family attribution rules of the Internal Revenue Service.

  - Cross-purchase agreements may not be effective for non-death trigger events. Owners have differing capacities to purchase stock of other owners when life insurance is not available for funding transactions.

  - This book does not focus on cross-purchase agreements. Nevertheless, agreements that use this format have all the same issues regarding non-death trigger events and valuation.

◉ **Entity-purchase agreements.** Entity-purchase agreements call for the corporation to purchase the shares upon the occurrence of trigger events. The entity (corporation) is then responsible for defining or providing the funding mechanism. Funding may be provided through the purchase of life insurance, financing by a third party or the selling shareholders, cash on hand, or a combination.

◉ **Hybrid agreements.** Hybrid agreements generally call for the entity to have the right of first refusal to purchase shares upon the occurrence of trigger events.

- In the event the corporation declines to purchase, it may have the right to offer the shares to the other shareholders pro rata or to selected shareholders.

- Hybrid agreements often give the corporation a "last look" if shares are first refused and other shareholders do not purchase the stock. For the hybrid agreement to be effective, the corporation's last look must be binding as to the purchase of the shares.

- Hybrid agreements can be used to create non-pro rata changes in relative ownership if that result is desired for business reasons. Funding may be through a combination of self-financing by the corporation, notes from selling shareholders, and life insurance.

For larger corporations, most buy-sell agreements are entity-purchase agreements, or they are hybrid in nature if the corporation has the right to allow individual shareholders to stand in its place. For substantial corporations with more than a few shareholders, the preponderance of buy-sell agreements are entity-purchase agreements, some of which may allow the redirection of purchases to some or all shareholders under specified circumstances. Nevertheless, the corporation almost always has the last look and requirement to purchase.

CROSS-PURCHASE COMPLEXITY

Cross-purchase agreements are often used in relatively small businesses with two or three shareholders, although there are exceptions to this statement. On the first line of Figure 2, assume A and B each own 50% of the business:

⊚   There are two shareholders.

⊚   There is one relationship.

⊚   If life insurance funds their buy-sell agreement, two policies will be required. (A buys a policy on B's life and B buys a policy on A's life.)

GROWING COMPLEXITY OF CROSS-PURCHASE AGREEMENTS LIMIT THEIR USEFULNESS		
# Shareholders	Shareholder Relationships	# Relationships / # Policies
2 (A and B)	AB	1 / 2
3 (A, B, and C)	AB BC AC	3 / 6
4 (A, B, C, and D)	AB AC AD BC BD CD	6 / 12
5 (A, B, C, D, and E)	AB AC AD AE BC BD BE CD CE DE	10 / 20
6 (A, B, C, D, E, and F)	You get the picture!	15 / 30

FIGURE 2

As Figure 2 illustrates, the number of relationships increases as the number of shareholders increases. The number of required insurance policies also increases proportionally. At some point, cross-purchase agreements become too cumbersome for reasonable operation.

> If your company began by developing one or more cross-purchase agreements, and now you have more owners, my challenge to you is to obtain appropriate legal and insurance advice to determine whether a company-owned life insurance program may be more appropriate for your situation.

CHAPTER EIGHT

TYPES OF BUY-SELL AGREEMENTS

Pete:	**"There are three main ways that prices are set for purposes of buy-sell agreements. There are agreements with fixed prices. Other agreements have formulas to determine the price. And finally, many agreements call for business appraisers to set the price in a valuation process. How is the price set in your agreement?"**
Sam:	"Well, when we signed our agreement 14 years ago, we agreed to set the value of the business at $4 million, so I guess we have a fixed-price agreement."
Pete:	**"Did you agree on that price formally as part of the buy-sell agreement?"**
Sam:	"Yes, we both signed off on that value and made it an exhibit to the agreement."
Pete:	**"Then you definitely have what is called a fixed-price agreement."**

The three categories of buy-sell agreements are cross-purchase agreements, entity agreements, and hybrid agreements. Buy-sell agreements can be placed into five general types based on the nature of the valuation mechanism:

- ⊚ **Fixed-price agreements.** Fixed-price agreements fix the price of future purchases at a specific dollar amount by stating a value for the equity of the enterprise, either in dollars or a per-share value. The shareholders agree on a fixed price and memorialize it, usually as an exhibit to the buy-sell agreement.

- ⊚ **Formula agreements.** Formula agreements provide a formula for determining value. Examples of formulas include a multiple of book value or earnings, or the agreement may call for an averaging of valuation indications developed using two or more formulas. The formula must be memorialized in the agreement.

- ⊚ **Shotgun agreements.** Shotgun agreements outline a process whereby one party offers to purchase (or sell) shares to another and the other party has the right (or the obligation) to sell (or purchase) the shares at the offered price. As with other types of buy-sell agreements, there are defined triggers indicating when one of the shareholders has the right to exercise the shotgun.

- ⊚ **Valuation process agreements.** Valuation process buy-sell agreements outline *valuation processes* through which future transactions will be priced. In nearly all cases, process agreements call upon the use of one or more business appraisers in the process of determining the price at which contemplated future transactions will occur. We divide process agreements into two categories because of important differences in how they operate:

  - • **Multiple appraiser agreements.** Multiple appraiser buy-sell agreements outline processes by which two or more appraisers are employed to determine value.

  - • **Single appraiser agreements.** Single appraiser buy-sell agreements outline processes by which a single appraiser is employed to determine value.

◉ **Rights of first refusal.** As we will see, rights of first refusal are sometimes considered to be a form of buy-sell agreement. However, they are not actually buy-sell agreements. More often, they are used in conjunction with buy-sell agreements.

Each type of buy-sell agreement has advantages and disadvantages. We address their relative benefits and detriments in the next several chapters.

EQUAL GOING IN. NOT EQUAL GOING OUT?

A group of individuals acquired 100% of the stock of a small company. Although the ownership of the business was not equal among them, there was no controlling shareholder, and each individual put up his proportionate share of the equity and guaranteed the original financing.

The shareholders entered into a buy-sell agreement that called for a valuation to be conducted following any trigger event. The agreement called for the selected appraiser to determine "the fair market value of the interest" owned by a deceased shareholder. During the next 10 years, the company grew, was profitable, and paid its acquisition debt in full. As a result, the value per share increased about 800% over the period. At this point, a shareholder who owned about 25% of the stock died unexpectedly.

I was retained as the single appraiser to provide the valuation that was to be determinative of value per the agreement. Early in the engagement, after reviewing a number of documents from the time of acquisition, I informed the company and the estate that there was a conflict between the language defining valuation in the buy-sell agreement and what appeared to be the intent of the parties:

◉ The buy-sell agreement called for the appraiser to determine "the fair market value of the interest."

    ⊚   Other documents from the acquisition period made it clear that the shareholders were "going into the deal equally, and would leave the deal equally," or at an enterprise level of value.

The estate's representative was not pleased with this news. The company was surprised at the language in the buy-sell agreement, but felt some responsibility to abide by the document. We requested, and the parties agreed, to adjust our assignment to provide opinions at both the marketable minority (enterprise) and the nonmarketable minority (interest) levels of value. Our valuation report provided these two opinions. The matter settled without litigation, fortunately, but could have been a disaster for all parties.

> **My challenge to you if your buy-sell agreement calls for a valuation process is, at a minimum, to have valuation-related language in your buy-sell agreement reviewed by a qualified business appraiser. Better yet, have an independent appraiser provide an appraisal to ensure that all parties understand the valuation process. Even better still, consider having an annual appraisal to update your buy-sell agreement and avoid problems like the above altogether.**

Chapter Nine

Fixed-Price
Buy-Sell Agreements

Pete: **"So you set the value of the business at $4 million when you set up your buy-sell agreement. Have you changed the price in the agreement since then?"**

Sam: "Sure. When William and Don came on board 10 years ago, we reset the price to value the company at $6 million. We updated that exhibit to the agreement at that time."

Pete: **"And how about since then?"**

Sam: "Ouch! We have not."

Pete: **"And what do you think the value of the business is today?"**

Sam: "I don't know for sure, but we have more than tripled sales and earnings since those younger guys joined us. I'd guess the business is worth $20 million, give or take a bit."

Pete: **"What would happen if you were to die tomorrow?"**

Sam: "The company could buy my stock for $2.4 million, or my 40% times the $6 million price in the agreement."

Pete: **"And, it is worth …?"**

Sam: "Maybe $8 million. I'm beginning to see what you're talking about."

Fixed-price buy-sell agreements do exactly what their name suggests – they fix a price today for transactions that will occur at future dates. Fixed-price agreements are often found in smaller corporations, partnerships, and LLCs.

Fixed-price agreements:

1. **Require agreement** *at a point in time* between shareholders of a corporation and/or the corporation. With a fixed-price agreement, the shareholders simply (or not so simply) agree on a price, which is memorialized in the agreement. The shareholders also agree on the other terms of its operation.

2. **Relate to transactions** that may or will occur *at future points in time* between the shareholders or between the shareholders and the corporation.

3. **Define the conditions** that will cause the buy-sell provisions to be triggered. These are the business and/or personal events that will trigger the operation of the buy-sell agreement.

4. **Determine the price** (for example, per share, per unit, or per member interest) at which the identified future transactions will occur. Fixed-price agreements often state that the agreed upon price will be updated periodically and that the agreed-upon price will be determinative of value until the time of the next updating.

Advantages

There are advantages to fixed-price agreements.

◉ **Easy to understand.** Once the price is agreed upon, everyone knows what the buy-sell price will be.

◉ **Easy to negotiate.** When fixed-price agreements are installed, there is often a common belief about the then-current value of the business (or business interest) among the shareholders. This may be the result of a recent transaction or of the capitalization of a startup operation.

⊚ **Inexpensive.** Fixed-price agreements often require minimal legal documentation regarding valuation than more complex agreements and other professionals – such as accountants and business appraisers – are utilized less frequently.

Disadvantages

The primary disadvantage of fixed-price agreements is *they are out of date shortly after they are inked.* We know one thing about the relationship of company value and time. Value changes over time, whether the result of corporate growth, favorable industry trends, good management decisions, or other factors on the favorable side. On the other hand, value can fall as result of corporate decline, unfavorable industry trends, bad management decisions, or other factors.

Virtually every fixed-price buy-sell agreement calls for the shareholders to revise their agreed-upon pricing, normally every year. While this may be the intention of the parties when an agreement is signed, fixed-price agreements are seldom updated on any regular schedule. In fact, there is never even an *original agreement* on price when some agreements are created.

It is sometimes easy for the parties to agree on the initial price for a fixed-price agreement. The agreement may be created at the time of a transaction or funding of the business and value is "visible." However, with the passage of time and in the absence of transactions or appraisals, value becomes much less visible.

As time goes by, it can become increasingly difficult and confrontational to discuss price. Such discussions force shareholders to consider their potential disabilities, firings, retirements, and even deaths.

Whether consciously or not, shareholders sometimes perceive the potential for personal advantage in the current fixed price:

⊚ Younger shareholders may perceive advantage in a dated, low (relative to current, actual value) buy-sell price if there are significant age or health differences relative to older owners.

⊚ Older shareholders may perceive advantage in a dated price if the fortunes of the company have declined and valuations are known to be generally lower than when the agreement was signed.

⊚ A healthy shareholder may perceive advantage if another owner is in poor health and disability or death provisions of the agreement may be triggered.

⊚ Optimistic shareholders may perceive advantage in that they do not believe that "bad things" could happen to them.

I don't want to attribute bad motives to good people. The problem with fixed-price agreements lies not with motives but with a natural divergence of interests and personal objectives over time. Revisit Figure 1, which shows potential opposing characteristics. Most business owners, at least in my experience, will go to extremes to avoid such discussions, which are often viewed with discomfort or as potentially antagonistic.

If there is a controlling shareholder and the remaining shareholders hold minority interests, it can become awkward to discuss valuation.

⊚ The minority shareholders are often thinking in terms of the value of the enterprise as a whole, and not in terms of illiquid, minority interests in the corporation.

⊚ The controlling shareholder may consider the minority shares to be worth proportionately less than his shares.

The end result is that all the shareholders – whether younger or older, in better or worse health, or having controlling or minority ownership – end up betting that something will happen to the other owner(s) first. *And one of them will be right.* Someone will win the bet and the other one(s) will lose it.

The problem with this scenario is that life is uncertain. People don't live or die or become disabled or leave based on the perceptions or expectations of others. They live or die according to a divine plan (if you are religious) or by chance, luck, or genes (if you are not). In any event, things happen over time, and they are not always the things we expect.

If you have younger and older shareholders, think about what would happen if a key younger shareholder died unexpectedly. What if an older owner with a substantial interest died? What about, heaven forbid, at least any time soon, you?

A Bad Cure

Some lawyers will advise against using a fixed-price agreement because they know of the almost universal tendency to fail to update them. Knowing this tendency, they sometimes suggest a potential cure for out-of-date pricing of fixed-price agreements. The so-called cure is a short clause calling for an appraisal process in the event the agreed-upon pricing is more than one year (or some period) old.

This solution might be workable, but the processes we have seen in such situations tend to be very short and lack the specification necessary to outline workable valuation processes. We'll learn more about this when we discuss process agreements.

Recommendation

My recommendation for companies with fixed-price buy-sell agreements is to revise or amend the agreement to provide for the following:

- Agreement by the company and all shareholders upon a qualified independent appraiser to provide an initial valuation for purposes of the agreement.

- This valuation would establish the price for the agreement until the next valuation, which would reset the price each year (or at least every other year).

- The parties could also agree there would be a valuation upon the occurrence of a trigger event more than a specified amount of time following the last valuation.

This is an overview of the *Single Appraiser, Select Now and Value Now* process described in Chapter 17. Chapter 17 is the core recommendation of this book. It calls for annual, or at least every other year, reappraisals for purposes of buy-sell agreements.

Some readers will have an initial reaction that the cost of a recurring valuation is too great for consideration. If that is your thought at this point, I would ask you to continue reading.

Conclusion

In my opinion, for most situations, fixed-price buy-sell agreements should be avoided like a contagious disease. However, if you have a fixed-price agreement, you must have the discipline to update the price periodically. And, you must amend the agreement to include a workable appraisal process in the (likely) event that you fail to update it.

THIS ONE DIDN'T WORK

The board of directors of a services firm prepared an initial valuation and updated it annually for purposes of the buy-sell agreement. They were not appraisers, but they did it themselves anyway. The genesis of the original valuation methodology was unclear. Examination of historical valuations indicated they were prepared at the strategic control level of value, i.e., as the company would be if purchased by a strategic buyer at each valuation date.

Perhaps this high level of valuation was impressive on the personal financial statements of the shareholders, all of whom were relatively young at the time (under 50 or so). The shareholders, like many of us, probably never gave a serious thought to the fact one of them might die.

A shareholder did die, quite unexpectedly, in a strange accident. His death invoked the shareholders' agreement, which called for his estate to be paid his pro rata share of the latest valuation. I was retained by the estate's representative to examine the buy-sell agreement and the latest valuations to determine if, in my opinion, the then-current valuation was fair from a financial point of view. The representative wanted to be sure there were no lurking problems with undervaluation.

There were no undervaluation problems. I found that the valuation per the shareholders' agreement was significantly in excess of the true pro rata value of the company's equity. Naturally, the mandatory sale by the estate to the company was fair to the estate. My finding would not have been the same had we been retained by the company.

If you insist on having a fixed-price buy-sell agreement, my challenge to you is to make sure the value is reasonable – both to the selling shareholder(s) and to the company. And make sure you have an ironclad, foolproof system to keep the price current as your business changes over time.

CHAPTER TEN

FORMULA
BUY-SELL AGREEMENTS

Pete:	"Some people think that a formula is the way to go to set the price for a buy-sell agreement. Did you guys ever consider using a formula to establish the price?"
Sam:	"We talked about using a formula, but things change so much in our industry that we were concerned that a static formula might not work for us. I've seen good companies in our business sell for less than 4 times earnings during recessions and for more than 6 times earnings during better times."
Pete:	"So you decided to update the value every year yourselves instead of risking the use of a formula?"
Sam:	"That's right. But that strategy hasn't seemed to work so well for us in retrospect. We had the best of intentions, but we just never seem to get around to resetting the price."

We define formula buy-sell agreements as agreements that define a formula for determining the pricing of transactions that occur following trigger events.

Companies (and their shareholders) with formula agreements may believe that these agreements are superior to fixed-price agreements. However, as we will see, formula agreements have their own issues. They fix a *single formula* today for transactions that will occur at future dates. We examine formula agreements through four key aspects of buy-sell agreements.

Formula agreements:

1. **Require agreement** *at a point in time* between shareholders of a corporation and/or the corporation. With a formula agreement, the shareholders simply (or not so simply) agree on a formula to determine price, which is memorialized in the agreement. Note that the "formula" can actually be a combination of formula calculations leading to a single result. An averaging of two calculations to achieve the final price would be an example of this.

2. **Relate to transactions** that may or will occur *at future points in time* between the shareholders or between the shareholders and the corporation.

3. **Define the conditions** that will cause the buy-sell provisions to be triggered. These are the business conditions that will trigger the operation of the buy-sell agreement, as well as the obligation of the company (or the shareholders) to repurchase the shares.

4. **Determine the price** (per share, per unit, or per member interest) at which the identified future transactions will occur. Formula agreements state a formula, which is typically applied to the then-current balance sheet or income statement metrics, to determine value. Some agreements call for the averaging of two or more separate calculations. Therefore, the series of calculations is the formula for those agreements. The formula can be changed over time by agreement of the parties. However, until such a change is made, the initial formula is normally determinative of value.

Advantages

As with other types of buy-sell agreements, formula agreements have certain advantages, including:

- **(Initially) Easy to understand.** Once the formula is selected, the specific calculations necessary to determine the buy-sell price are known. Some typical formulas include multiples of net income, pre-tax income, operating income, and earnings before interest, taxes, depreciation and amortization (EBITDA). These formulas refer to what is called the *capitalization of earnings*. Book value (or a multiple of book value) is sometimes used as well.

- **Easy to negotiate.** When a formula agreement is installed, there is generally a common belief among the shareholders about the then-current value of the business. The value is effectively converted into the formula.

- **Inexpensive.** Formula agreements require less legal documentation and do not require the use of valuation professionals, unless a valuation professional is used to assist in developing the formula.

Disadvantages

Formula buy-sell agreements also have certain disadvantages. My experience suggests that no formula selected at a given time can consistently provide reasonable and realistic valuations over time. This is true because of the myriad changes that occur within individual companies, local or regional economies, the national economy, and within industries. Formulas simply cannot take into account these many factors in a meaningful and consistent manner.

Two kinds of formulas are often used in buy-sell agreements. The first kind is based on book value. The second kind is based on a multiple of some measure of earnings. Some formulas actually call for a combination of the two kinds. We address each kind of formula below.

Formulas Related to Book Value

The use of book value is one of the most common formulas. Nevertheless, it is one of the least effective. If the owners of a company invest $1 million in the business at the outset, book value may be the best formula for determining value *at that moment*. However, that same book value formula would not be effective if there are expectations of operating losses prior to achieving profitability. Value will, in fact, be equal to a company's book value only by chance after it has been in operation for some time.

Formulas Related to Earnings

One summary representation of business value, i.e., a generalized formula, can be expressed as:

$$Value = Earnings \; x \; Multiple$$

To develop a formula for a buy-sell agreement, all one has to do is to decide on the appropriate measure of earnings, and then the appropriate multiple to be applied to that earnings measure (i.e., with which to *capitalize* the earnings). As I have said in many speeches, if valuation were that simple, appraisers would not be necessary.

Possible Formulas and Future Earnings Patterns

The purpose of the analysis and tables that follow is not to try to illustrate any particular formula. Rather, it is included to illustrate the complexity that underlies the use of formulas. As is quickly seen, the use of formulas is not simple.

The analysis in Figures 3 and 4 considers different formulas based on earnings and different earnings multiples, all of which could be, at different points in time, reasonably reflective of value for a given enterprise. Assume we are discussing pre-tax earnings.

Examples of an earnings scenario that reflects rising earnings is presented in Figure 3, along with six possible weights that might be assigned to combinations of historical or expected earnings. Normally, a business appraiser would select something like one of these combinations while conducting an appraisal. His choice would be informed by the facts and circumstances in existence at the valuation date.

	Prior Year 3	Prior Year 2	Prior Year 1	Most Recent Year
Pre-Tax Earnings	$700	$800	$900	$1,000
Weights				
A				1
B			1	1
C		1	1	1
D	1	1	1	1
E		1	2	3
F	1	2	3	4

FIGURE 3

If you use an earnings capitalization formula, chances are it will be something like one of the above weighting schemes applied to some measure of earnings. The problem is that facts and circumstances change over time, and the formula you select when you sign your agreement may not be appropriate at a future trigger event.

Possible Multiples

If you use a multiple of earnings formula method, you have to select a multiple. Multiples change over time in most industries based on industry conditions, interest rates, availability of financing, the economy, the stock market, and company-specific factors.

You be the judge. Assume for the moment that the appropriate earnings multiple is in the range of four to six times the selected measure of earnings. Figure 4 illustrates the range of possible conclusions of value based on the six different weighting scenarios and the range of multiples from four to six times the earnings for steadily growing earnings.

				Low to High
Pre-Tax Multiples of EBITDA	4.0	5.0	6.0	50%
Pre-Tax Earnings	$700	$800	$900	$1,000	43%
	Weighted Avg. Earnings	Implied Values		
A	$1,000	$4,000	$5,000	$6,000
B	$950	$3,800	$4,750	$5,700
C	$900	$3,600	$4,500	$5,400
D	$850	$3,400	$4,250	$5,100
E	$933	$3,733	$4,667	$5,600
F	$900	$3,600	$4,500	$5,400
Minimums	$850	$3,400	$4,250	$5,100
Maximums	$1,000	$4,000	$5,000	$6,000
Low to High	18%	76%		

FIGURE 4

We make the following observations from Figure 4:

⊚ **Pre-tax earnings.** Earnings rise steadily from $700 to $1,000 over the four years shown, or a total of 43%.

⊙ **The multiple.** The range of four to six for the selected multiple of pre-tax earnings indicates a 50% swing from low to high. Multiples change over time, so the selection of any single multiple for a formula today might be wrong relative to the market, by as much as 50% (or more or less) based solely on that selection.

⊙ **The weightings.** The range of calculated values for any given multiple indicates an 18% swing from minimum to maximum (i.e., from the minimum weighted average of $850 to the maximum weighted average of $1,000).

⊙ **In combination.** The combination of variations in multiples and weightings indicates a swing of 76% from the lowest value ($3.4 million) to the highest ($6.0 million).

Keep in mind, Figure 4 shows the range of weighted earnings and multiples based on steadily rising earnings. The range of value conclusions might be even greater if expected earnings are variable.

If you have but one chance to select the appropriate valuation mechanism at a future date from the figures above, which would you pick? Might there not be a better way to decide the pricing mechanism for your buy-sell agreement?

Other Caveats for Formula Agreements

It is one thing to think you understand a formula. It is quite another to write it down so that those who are called upon to calculate its intended value will understand exactly what the parties meant when the formula agreement was signed. As an example, review the following example formula that might be found in a buy-sell agreement:

1. The corporation's earnings before interest, taxes, depreciation, and amortization (EBITDA) for the trailing

12 months ending the month-end prior to the event giving rise to the required transaction ("the Determination Date") shall be calculated by the corporation's outside accountant. EBITDA will be multiplied by a multiple of 5.0. The product of the calculated EBITDA and 5.0 will represent the market value of the total capital of the business (MVTC).

2. From the MVTC of the business, the interest-bearing debt (IBD) outstanding on the balance sheet as of the month-end immediately prior to the event giving rise to the required transaction will be subtracted with the difference representing the market value of the equity of the business (MVE).

3. The MVE of the business will be divided by the number of shares outstanding as of the Determination Date (Shares Outstanding, or SO), with the result being MVE per share.

4. MVE per share will be multiplied by the number of shares subject to the required transaction (Shares to be Purchased, or SP), with the result being the amount due to the selling shareholder (the Due Amount, or DA) from the corporation under terms to be specified.

5. The Due Amount will therefore be calculated by the following formula:

$$DA = (((EBITDA \times 5.0) - IBD) / SO) \times SP$$

6. The Due Amount shall be calculated by the corporation's independent certified public accountant within 30 days of the Determination Date.

If you have a formula agreement, I suggest that the language be written in your agreement in explicit terms as indicated above. Further, the actual formula should also be stated algebraically. And finally, the formula should be calculated and appended to the agreement to ensure its clarity and consistent application.

As an example, assume the following as of the Determination Date:

1. EBITDA, as calculated by the corporation's outside accountant is $10 million for the trailing 12 months ending closest to the Determination Date.

2. Interest-bearing debt (IBD) totals $5 million as of the month-end prior to the Determination Date.

3. Shares Outstanding, or SO, as of the Determination Date are 1 million shares.

4. The Shares to be Purchased, or SP, equals 10% of the Shares Outstanding, or 100,000 shares.

The corporation's outside accountant calculates the Due Amount as follows:

$$DA = (((\$10,000,000 \times 5.0) - \$5,000,000) / 1,000,000) \times 100,000$$

$$= ((\$50,000,000 - \$5,000,000) / 1,000,000) \times 100,000$$

$$= \$45 \text{ per share} \times 100,000 \text{ shares}$$

$$= \$4,500,000$$

While the algebra may seem frightening to the math-impaired, it is actually fairly straightforward. Therein is the attractiveness of formula buy-sell agreements. They are conceptually easy to understand and, supposedly, not difficult to implement.

Should the selling shareholder be happy with the resulting calculation? Let's dig a bit further.

⊚   What if we learned that EBITDA, but for a one-time charge to write down stale inventory, would have been $12 million rather than $10 million? If an adjustment were made for this nonrecurring item, which would be routine in most appraisals, the resulting Due Amount would have been $5.5 million.

⊚ What if the corporation had $5 million of excess cash on its balance sheet (with earnings of $10 million)? The Due Amount would have been $5 million. Under these circumstances, the selling shareholder would likely be quite upset if he or she was offered only $4.5 million for his or her shares. However, given the language of the agreement, he or she might have no right to the pro rata share of excess assets accumulated (i.e., not distributed) during his or her tenure as a shareholder.

I have seen formula agreements in which the company's accountant or other advisor calculated the original formula pricing for the agreement. The calculations were then appended to the buy-sell agreements as exhibits. In some cases, the accountant made certain adjustments that are not mentioned in the agreement itself. The concept of adjustments to a formula pricing mechanism raises important questions:

⊚ Should the person making the calculation for purposes of the agreement make the exact same adjustments at every future calculation date?

⊚ Should he or she update those adjustments to the current pricing date?

⊚ Should he or she consider other possible adjustments that make sense at a new determination date, even though they are neither in the original calculation or the agreement itself?

While the example called for the company's independent accountant to make the calculation, some agreements do not specify who should make it. If the person is not named, then presumably anyone could make the calculation. What would happen if the corporation's controller made one calculation and an accountant retained by the selling shareholder made another – and the two were materially different in their conclusions?

Situations like the above in which the application of formula pricing yields a conclusion obviously different from actual economic value, or where there is potential for disagreement regarding the calculation, create the potential for litigation, unhappiness, anger, loss of friendships, and many other unfavorable results.

Needless to say, we do not recommend the use of formulas in corporate buy-sell agreements.

Recommendation

My recommendation for companies with formula buy-sell agreements is that to revise or amend the agreement to provide for the following:

- Agreement by the company and all shareholders upon a qualified independent appraiser to provide an initial valuation for purposes of the agreement.

- This valuation would establish the price for the agreement until the next valuation, which would reset the price each year (or at least every other year).

- The parties could also agree there would be a valuation upon the occurrence of a trigger event more than a specified amount of time following the last valuation.

This process is an overview of the *Single Appraiser, Select Now and Value Now* process (the core recommendation of this book) described in Chapter 17. It calls for annual, or at least every other year, reappraisals for purposes of buy-sell agreements.

BOOK VALUE AS THE "FORMULA"

For additional perspective, we offer the following comments on the use of book value in buy-sell agreements from Richard M. Wise, FASA, MCBA, FCBV, FCA, a prominent Canadian business appraiser.[3]

> "Book value" (which would generally be at historical cost) may be totally inappropriate in determining price in a buy-sell agreement and unfair as a basis for the acquisition of the terminating shareholder's shares. Either the continuing shareholder(s) or the terminating shareholder will be unfairly treated if the buy-sell price is book value (except perhaps in portfolio investment-type situations)...
>
> "Book value" has several other important shortcomings when it is used for purposes of setting the buy-sell price. Consider the result in each of the following unrelated hypothetical situations:
>
> • A business has substantial earnings power, and goodwill is not reflected on the balance sheet. Moreover, the terminating shareholder was instrumental in creating and maintaining the goodwill.
>
> • There are various potential liabilities (distinct from contingent liabilities) such as letters of credit available but not yet presented to or paid by the bank, environmental considerations, etc.
>
> • At the time of the signing of the agreement, the circumstances were different from those prevailing when the triggering event occurs.

---

3   Wise, Richard M., "Valuation Aspects of Shareholders' Buy-Sell Agreements," *Business Valuation Review,* March 2005, Vol. 24, No. 1, pp. 6-12.

- Accounting policies such as the capitalization of certain repairs or the treatment of depreciation, etc. have not been consistent from year to year since the signing of the buy-sell agreement.

- The company is on a cash basis of accounting rather than on an accrual basis.

- There are pending lawsuits or substantial claims by or against the company (referred to in the notes to the financial statements), and it is impossible to determine their potential outcome.

- There are inventory and other hidden reserves.

- The company's balance sheet reflects purchased goodwill which has lost value since acquisition and has not yet been written down pursuant to the annual impairment test under GAAP.

- The specified event is death, and life insurance proceeds will be payable to the company as beneficiary and owner of the policy.

- The company is the guarantor of bank loans to a third party.

- There are product warranties outstanding which have not been booked (but only noted) on the financial statements.

- There is long-term debt owing to arm's-length creditors, but bearing interest at rates substantially below current market rates on similar obligations.

Mr. Wise concludes: "In summary, although 'book value' may be the simplest term to understand – and to calculate – it will often yield unfair results." My challenge to you is to understand the pitfalls of even the seemingly most simple formula.

CHAPTER ELEVEN

SHOTGUN AGREEMENTS

Pete:	**"Have you ever heard of a shotgun agreement for setting price for buy-sell agreements?"**
Sam:	"Yes. Our attorney suggested we try that when we first got started."
Pete:	**"Why didn't you do it?"**
Sam:	"Well, I talked that over with my wife and she said 'No way!' She didn't want either end of a shotgun if something happened to me."
Pete:	**"That shows a lot of insight on her part."**
Sam:	"I've always said she's the brains of our partnership."

Shotgun agreements are found in some buy-sell agreements, but we do not see them very often. A shotgun buy-sell agreement is an agreement where, upon the occurrence of a trigger event, one party or the other makes a determination of price and the other party is able to buy or sell at that price. They are often used to provide a way to break deadlock situations between owners. These agreements:

1. **Require agreement** *at a point in time,* usually between shareholders of a corporation, or else between corporate joint venture partners.

2. **Relate to transactions** that may or will occur *at future points in time* between the shareholders, or between the

shareholders and corporate joint venture partners, or between corporate joint venture partners.

3. **Define the conditions** that will cause the buy-sell provisions to be triggered. These are the business conditions that will trigger the operation of the buy-sell agreement, and the obligation to purchase shares pursuant to the agreement.

4. **Determine the price** (per share, per unit, or per member interest) at which the identified future transactions will occur. The shotgun process will determine the price at which future transactions will occur, but no one knows until an offer is made what that price will be. One version of a shotgun agreement might require that:

    •   One party is called upon to offer a price at which he or she will buy or sell.

    •   The other party then has the right to buy or sell at that price.

    •   In either event, the "shotgun" aspect of the agreement requires that there be a transaction, but the initial party does not know whether he or she will be a seller or a buyer at the time the offer is made.

    •   The concept is quite simple. The initial offering side (which will that be?) virtually has to name a reasonable price, since it is a price at which that side must be willing to sell or to buy. However, there are two implicit assumptions with these agreements that may not be met:

        •   Both sides have sufficient financial capacity to engage in the transaction, and

        •   Both sides are sufficiently knowledgeable about the business and are able to make an informed offer, or to evaluate the offer made.

Advantages

As with formula and fixed-price agreements, shotgun agreements appear simple. Advantages include:

1. **Easy to understand.** Once the shotgun mechanism is decided upon, the parties know that it may be invoked at a point in the future upon the occurrence of a trigger event.

2. **Easy to negotiate.** The logic of shotguns can seem compelling. All we have to do today is to agree that one party will have to name a price at which they will be willing to sell or to buy, and the other party has to similarly agree that they will buy or sell at that named price.

3. **Inexpensive.** The agreement requires less legal documentation and no appraisers to determine the price.

4. **Pressure for reasonable price.** As we have already noted, there should be pressure on the initial offering party to establish a reasonable price.

Disadvantages

There are some disadvantages to shotgun buy-sell agreements.

1. **Implicit assumptions may not hold.** The parties seldom have equal financial capacities and may have different knowledge about the business. For example, a nonoperating shareholder may be at a distinct disadvantage in terms of making an offer to buy. Assume there are two operating partners, each owning 50%. Certainly a shotgun agreement is fair, or is it? Assume further that one partner dies. The surviving spouse is not active in management and might be at a distinct disadvantage.

2.   **Minority shareholders may be at a disadvantage.** It is easier for a 90% shareholder to acquire a 10% interest than vice versa. A smaller shareholder, unable to swing the big deal, may have to offer a relatively low price in order to ensure his/her capability to either buy or sell, thereby increasing the odds that the other side will buy.

3.   **Uncertainty as to final outcome.** Relative to fixed-price and formula agreements, there is great uncertainty as to what will happen when a shotgun agreement is triggered. Sellers usually don't want to become buyers, or vice versa.

Parties engaging in shotgun agreements need to be sure they have thought through the implications of a trigger event under all reasonably possible scenarios. Even if this is done, I am hard-pressed to think of an ideal situation for a shotgun buy-sell agreement. The first exception that comes to mind might involve large corporate venture partners. However, even with such partners, one would be at a distinct disadvantage relative to the other if it were undergoing difficult financial circumstances at the time of a trigger event.

THE OTHER GUY WON'T ALWAYS BE FIRST TO GO

When drafting your buy-sell agreement, understand that the other guy will not always be the first to die or to leave the company. It might be you. However, your buy-sell agreement is indifferent to timing. It will apply to you (and the other owners) whether you become a buyer or a seller.

If you know you will be a buyer, then you would likely prefer to buy at the lowest possible price. If you know you will be a seller, then you probably would prefer to sell at the highest possible price. If you don't know which you will be (and you likely do not) and you act rationally, you will desire pricing in the buy-sell agreement that is reasonable regardless of future outcomes.

Applying similar logic with the other shareholders to other aspects of your buy-sell agreement leads to workable agreements. Failing to apply this kind of logic may embed traps in the agreement for one side and potential advantages for the other side. You just don't know which side you will be on when a trigger event happens.

It is important to talk about the future when the interests of the parties are aligned, or at least not sufficiently misaligned to prevent discussion.

My challenge to you is to make time to work out important issues when drafting the agreement. Know this for certain: When your buy-sell agreement is triggered, the interests of the parties will have diverged and agreement will be difficult, or even impossible, to reach.

CHAPTER TWELVE

RIGHTS OF FIRST REFUSAL

Pete:	**"Do you know what a right of first refusal is?"**
Sam:	"I think so. Isn't that when a shareholder can't sell to someone outside the owner group without first giving the other owners a chance to buy his shares?"
Pete:	**"That's the basic idea. Does your buy-sell agreement have a right of first refusal section in it?"**
Sam:	"I don't think so. When it was just George and me, we didn't think we'd need something like that. I remember that it offended George that I might even consider such a thing. I do remember that our accountant suggested we add a right of first refusal to our buy-sell agreement when William and Don joined us, but we never got around to it."
Pete:	**"Let's keep on. We're learning a lot about your buy-sell agreement. And we're learning that it does have some problems. Stay with me a while longer and we'll get you in a position to begin to get your agreement fixed!"**

How They Work

Rights of first refusal (ROFRs) are sometimes considered to be a form of buy-sell agreement. A right of first refusal is an agreement designed, for the most part, to restrict ownership of shares by limiting their marketability. The typical right of first refusal states the conditions under which shares of a corporation can be sold. Rights of first refusal tend to work along these lines.

1. If a shareholder desires to sell his or her shares to a third party and the third party provides a concrete offer, then the corporation retains a right of first refusal to purchase the shares at the same price and on the same terms offered to the existing shareholder by the third party. The corporation generally has a period of time, from 30 to 60 days or more, during which to match the third party offer and purchase the subject shares.

2. If the corporation does not match the offer within the specified period, many agreements provide what could be called a "right of second refusal" to the other shareholders of the corporation. Such secondary rights are normally offered to the shareholders pro rata to their existing ownership. If one or more shareholders elect not to purchase, the other shareholders can then purchase the extra shares (usually pro rata to remaining ownership). The other shareholders then have a period of time, from 30 to 60 days or more, during which to match the third party offer and purchase the subject shares.

3. In order to ensure the possibility of a completed transaction, the corporation must have a "last look" opportunity to purchase the shares if the other shareholders do not. The corporation is granted some additional time – perhaps 30 to 60 days or so – to make this final decision.

4. If all of the prior rights are refused, then and only then, is the original shareholder allowed to sell his or her shares to the third party – again, at the price and terms shown to the company and other shareholders. At that point, the buying party is normally required to agree to become subject to the very same right of first refusal – and buy-sell agreement – that hindered his purchase.

What They Do

Rights of first refusal are not the same as buy-sell agreements. They may seem to operate like a buy-sell agreement, in that they provide procedures related to possible future stock transactions. But ROFRs do not ensure transactions will occur.

Rights of first refusal restrict the marketability of shares during the period of time shareholders own stock in a corporation. They restrict marketability because they discourage third parties from engaging in the time, effort, and expense of due diligence regarding investments. Rights of first refusal often add months to the time a transaction could occur, and they create great uncertainty for potential third party buyers, as well as for selling shareholders.

Rights of first refusal are designed to do several things from the viewpoint of a corporation and remaining shareholders:

⊚ They discourage third parties from making offers to buy shares from individual shareholders.

⊚ They also give the corporation control over the inclusion of third parties as new shareholders.

⊚ If a third party offer is low relative to intrinsic value as perceived by the corporation and the other shareholders, the third party will know (or likely believe) there is a high likelihood the offer will be matched by either the corporation or the other shareholders, so there is little opportunity to purchase shares at a bargain price.

- If a third party offer is at the level of perceived intrinsic value, the corporation and/or the shareholders are likely to purchase the shares if there is any likelihood that they do not want to be in business with the third party.

- Additionally, if the third party offer is in excess of perceived intrinsic value and the corporation does allow the third party as a shareholder, the third party almost certainly knows he or she is paying more than either the corporation or any of its shareholders believed the shares to be worth.

- Finally, most ROFRs require any successful third party purchaser to agree to become subject to the same (restrictive) agreement.

Agreements including ROFRs are often written so shareholders can sell shares to each other (often requiring such transactions do not impact control of the entity), or transfer shares within their families. These provisions provide flexibility for shareholders who are "on the team," so to speak.

The bottom line about rights of first refusal is they restrict marketability. ROFRs can affect the fair market value of illiquid, minority interests in private companies. Business appraisers take the incremental risks associated with such provisions into account when determining the size of applicable marketability discounts.

Buy-sell agreements provide for marketability under specified terms and conditions upon the occurrence of specified trigger events.

LOSING A PARTNER? DON'T LOSE THE BUSINESS

San Francisco wealth manager, Jonathan DeYoe, wrote in the *San Francisco East Bay Express*:

> You have no doubt heard the expression "not making a decision is a decision." When I am talking to a client who is a partner in a successful business venture, I like to modify the saying in this manner: "Not having a plan is a plan ... and not a very good one."

And, further,

> You have to work hard to build a successful business. Before you decide not to make a decision about putting together a buy-sell agreement, think again. Not having a plan may be a plan, but you, your partners, your family, and your business deserve better.

My challenge to you is to have a plan and a buy-sell agreement so that the unexpected death or departure of a substantial owner won't derail the business. On the one hand, no one may want to purchase the interest, particularly if it is a minority interest. Absent a plan for liquidity, the deceased shareholder's estate may not be a good owner. On the other hand, there may be interested parties for the block of stock that you would prefer, or even strongly prefer, not to have as shareholders. In either case, the company needs a plan.

PART III

VALUATION PROCESS BUY-SELL AGREEMENTS

CHAPTER THIRTEEN

VALUATION PROCESS BUY-SELL AGREEMENTS AND THEIR DEFINING ELEMENTS

Pete:	**"Have you ever heard of a buy-sell agreement where there is an appraisal process to establish the price?"**
Sam:	"Yes. A number of my friends have mentioned that their agreements work that way."
Pete:	**"Did you guys ever consider a valuation process for your agreement?"**
Sam:	"Not really. But, wait! When we told our attorney that we were going to set the price for our agreement, he asked us what we would do if we hadn't agreed on an updated price and the fixed-price was way out of date. We said we didn't know. So he put a paragraph in the agreement to fix that problem."
Pete:	**"What do you mean?"**
Sam:	"Well, there's a paragraph in this agreement somewhere that says something about us hiring appraisers if the price in the agreement is more than two years old and, as you say, the agreement is 'triggered' for some reason. Maybe I'd get a better value than the $6 million fixed price after all!"

Pete:	**"Do you know how that process would work?"**
Sam:	"Actually, I don't have a clue."
Pete:	**"That brings us to a critical point in our discussion. I told you at dinner the other night that I knew your buy-sell agreement had problems. You didn't believe me, did you?"**
Sam:	"Well, I had a vague suspicion about a few things, particularly about not having updated the price in the agreement. But no, I didn't really believe you."
Pete:	**"Do you believe me now?"**
Sam:	"Yup, I do. I know that the fixed-price deal is not working. We don't have a right of first refusal, so basically, anyone can do pretty much what they please with the stock, regardless of what the rest of us think. I don't have the foggiest idea of what happens if someone gets divorced, and William is not in a good family situation right now. If something happens now, the price might be set by some appraisers, and we don't know who they are or what the process is or what kind of value they might reach. Other than that, I guess, our agreement is in pretty good shape!"
Pete:	**"Don't be hard on yourself. As they say, forewarned is forearmed. I can't tell you how many buy-sell agreements have the same problems and many more. The bottom line is that we tend to avoid thinking about them because we don't like to think about unpleasant things. And many owners, like you and George, avoid talking about their agreements like they are a plague."**
Sam:	"That pretty much describes our situation."

Pete:	"Let's focus on one other thing now. If a shareholder dies and there isn't enough life insurance to purchase the stock at a trigger event, what happens?"
Sam:	"The company will issue a note for the balance."
Pete:	"What are the terms of the note?"
Sam:	"Well, let's see. The company has to pay 20% of the difference at closing, and then the rest is paid out over 10 years."
Pete:	"What's the interest rate?"
Sam:	"Well, it says the note will pay interest at the prime rate of our local bank or its successor."
Pete:	"Is that fixed at the time the note is created or does the rate float?"
Sam:	"It doesn't say."
Pete:	"Could that make a difference to the company or to a shareholder or his estate?"
Sam:	"You bet it could."
Pete:	"And what security does a note holder have?"
Sam:	"Well, Pete, once again, it doesn't say."
Pete:	"So that means none. Right?"
Sam:	"I guess so. We do have a lot to work on."

Valuation Process Agreements

Valuation process buy-sell agreements, or agreements where a valuation process is used to establish value, share certain commonalities. Valuation process agreements:

1. **Require agreement** *at a point in time* between shareholders of a corporation and/or the corporation. With a valuation process agreement, the shareholders and the corporation reach agreement about the process that will determine the price (valuation) for future transactions rather than stating a particular price or formula.

2. **Relate to transactions** that may or will occur *at future points in time* between the shareholders, or between the shareholders and the corporation.

3. **Define the conditions** that will cause the buy-sell provisions to be triggered. These are the business conditions that will trigger the operation of the buy-sell agreement and the obligation to purchase shares pursuant to the agreement.

4. **Determine the price** (per share, per unit, or per member interest) at which the identified future transactions will occur. The process, usually involving one or more appraisers, determines the price for future transactions.

There are two kinds of valuation process buy-sell agreements: multiple appraiser agreements and single appraiser agreements.

- **Multiple appraiser agreements** utilize two or more appraisers who provide appraisals that are designed to determine the agreement price. They come in a variety of forms, which we will discuss. They also come with substantial disadvantages that, in my opinion, are usually outweighed by their apparent advantages.

- ⊚ **Single appraiser process agreements** utilize a single appraiser to determine the agreement price. As I've suggested before, and will reiterate, the single appraiser process agreement provides the best available valuation process for most closely held businesses to determine the price(s) for their buy-sell agreements.

Whether yours is a multiple or single appraiser agreement, a definition of the assignment is needed in order for the appraisers to determine the price. Let me be more specific. *If you want appraisers to determine the price for your buy-sell agreement, you have to tell them what kind of price you want!*

The Defining Elements of Valuation Process Agreements

We'll go into the individual components of what "kind of price" means, but an initial overview is helpful. Five critical elements must be defined if you want an appraiser to provide a valuation for your buy-sell agreement. A sixth element is so important from a business perspective that we include it as an additional defining element.

1. Standard of Value	4. Qualifications of Appraisers
2. Level of Value	5. Appraisal Standards
3. The "As Of" Date	6. Funding Mechanisms

If you don't tell the business appraisers what you want for each of these elements, *they will decide for you!* Why? Because each of the first five elements *is required* to specify an appraisal that will follow prevailing business appraisal standards – and you certainly want your appraiser to follow appropriate standards.

Let's begin with a brief overview of the first five defining elements, and elaborate on them in the following chapters.

1. **Standard of value.** The standard of value is the identification of the type of value to be used in a specific appraisal (or valuation) engagement. The proper identification of the standard of value is the cornerstone of every valuation. The parties to the agreement (that's you and your fellow owners) should select that standard of value. If you don't, the appraisers will have to select it for you – and you may not like their choices.

    Will value be based on "fair market value," "fair value," or some other standard? These words can result in dramatically different interpretations from a valuation perspective. Some agreements simply specify "the value" of the company or interest, which is not adequate to define the standard of value. The likelihood of a successful appraisal process falls to near zero if the standard of value is not clearly specified.

2. **Level of value.** Will the value be based on a *pro rata share of the value of the business* or will it be based on the *value of a particular interest in the business?* This distinction is critical to any appraisal process – and to the owners of your business who are parties to your buy-sell agreement. Again, if you don't make a knowledgeable choice, someone else (the appraisers) will make it for – or against – you. There is no presumption of malice or lack of independence in this statement. The problem is that many agreements are written such that they are subject to differing interpretations regarding the appropriate level of value.

    The differences bring into play things appraisers call "minority interest discounts" and "marketability discounts." A discounted value will always be lower than an undiscounted value. The reason you want to specify the level of value is that, if you decide discounts are okay, then that level defines the rate from which the discounts are to be taken. That's pretty much common sense.

Two appraisers could agree on the total value of a business, but if one applies a minority interest discount or a marketability discount, their conclusions may be *hugely different*. This is not surprising because their conclusions represent two different levels of value. One appraiser will have valued the business, while the other will have valued an interest in the business. The desired level of value needs to be crystal clear in your agreement.

3. **The "as of" date for the valuation.** Every appraisal is grounded at a point in time. That time – referred to as the "valuation date," "effective date," or "as of" date – provides the perspective, whether current or historical, from which the appraisal is prepared. Unfortunately, some buy-sell agreements are not clear about the date on which the valuation(s) should be determined by appraisers. This can be extremely important, particularly in corporate partnerships and joint ventures when trigger events establish the valuation date. Because value changes over time, it is essential that the "as of" date be specified.

4. **Qualifications of appraisers.** If you don't decide on the kind of appraiser(s) you want to help with your buy-sell agreement, then, unfortunately, almost anyone can be named by you or other parties to your agreement. Do you want a college professor who has never done an appraisal as your appraiser? How about an accountant who has no business valuation training? How about a broker who has no business valuation experience unrelated to transactions? Or how about a shareholder's brother who

has an MBA but has never valued a business before? You get the picture. Your buy-sell agreement has to specify the qualifications of appraisers who may be called if your agreement is triggered.

One way to solve this problem, which we'll discuss shortly, is for all of the owners and the company to agree on a *qualified independent appraiser* before you sign your agreement. Unfortunately, many buy-sell agreements are silent on this issue. Absent clear specification of the appraiser qualifications, there is no assurance that appraisers considered for buy-sell valuations will be qualified to provide the required services. And rest assured that after a triggering event, the interests will diverge among the shareholder who has been triggered, the other shareholders, and the company. Getting agreement may be virtually impossible.

5. **Appraisal standards to be followed.** Some buy-sell agreements go so far as to name the specific business appraisal standards that must be followed by the appraisers. Business appraisal standards provide minimum standards (criteria) to be followed by business appraisers in conducting and reporting their appraisals. And you certainly want your appraiser to follow minimum standards!

Some agreements state that the appraiser(s) must follow the *Uniform Standards of Professional Appraisal Practice*, the *ASA Business Valuation Standards of the American Society of Appraisers*, or other standards. Other agreements might state that the appraiser(s) must follow the AICPA's *Statement on Standards for Valuation Services No. 1 (SSVS-1)*, or other sets of standards. Your buy-sell agreement should do so as well.

What's so hard about specifying these defining elements? Getting specific often makes people *talk about* things they don't even want to *think about*. But think about them they must. If you think it is difficult to address these issues with your partner(s) in the *here and now*, just think how difficult it will be when one of you is in the *hereafter*.

Know this: If these defining elements are unclear in your buy-sell agreement, then they may be the only thing you will be able to think about following a trigger event, until the situation is resolved. Absent a clear agreement, this can take lots of money and time, and create lots of hard feelings. In addition, dealing with these issues under adverse circumstances will absolutely distract you from running your business.

Overview of Funding Mechanisms

A buy-sell agreement is no better than its funding mechanism, which is necessary to ensure its workability from the viewpoints of both future buyers and sellers.

1. Standard of Value	4. Qualifications of Appraisers
2. Level of Value	5. Appraisal Standards
3. The "As Of" Date	6. Funding Mechanisms

The sixth defining element relates to the funding of buy-sell agreements.

6. **The funding mechanism(s).** The funding mechanism is thought of separately from valuation. However, there may be interrelationships between the valuation and the funding mechanism that should be considered in your buy-sell agreement. For example, your company may have life insurance on the lives of its shareholders. If an owner dies, what happens to the life insurance? Does the

agreement specify the use of life insurance proceeds? A failure to treat insurance proceeds clearly in a buy-sell agreement could lead to different treatments for purposes of the agreement and for estate tax purposes. This would not be a good result!

And does the agreement tell the appraisers how you want them to treat the proceeds in their valuations? Does the agreement provide for the company to issue a note to a deceased or departed shareholder? If so, what are the terms of the note?

An agreement is no better than the ability of the parties and/or the company to fund any required purchases at the agreed-upon price. An agreement that is silent can be like having no agreement at all. We discuss funding mechanisms further below. Chapter 15 discusses the treatment of life insurance proceeds in greater detail. If your buy-sell agreement has associated life insurance, you may want to review that chapter carefully.

As a general rule, life insurance policy payments are not tax deductible. The non-tax deductibility of life insurance payments can create pass-through income for shareholders of S corporations, and owners in partnerships and limited liability companies. If your company is purchasing life insurance for purposes of your buy-sell agreement, it is a good idea to discuss with your accountant or tax attorney the tax consequences of policy ownership on shareholders or other pass-through owners.

The corollary to the non-deductibility of life insurance costs is that, as a general rule, the proceeds of life insurance policies are not taxable. There can sometimes be issues with alternative minimum taxes. Again, it is a good idea to talk about your life insurance issues with your accountant or tax attorney. The rules are, as they say, what they are (and certainly beyond my expertise). Nevertheless, you don't want to be surprised with unexpected tax bills from the operation of your buy-sell agreement.

As mentioned, the funding mechanism is not actually necessary to define the engagement for valuation purposes and has nothing to do with appraisal standards or qualifications. What the funding mechanism does, however, is provide that the agreed-upon value will first, be *affordable to the company,* and second, *realizable by the selling shareholder.* The funding mechanism, then, is an essential business element of buy-sell agreements.

There is a natural tension between the buyer and seller over the pricing and terms of buy-sell transactions. This tension is illustrated in Figure 5.

BUYER-SELLER TENSIONS

	Buyer (Company)	Seller (Shareholder)
Price	Low	High
Terms	Lenient *Long Term* *Deferred Payments* *Low Interest Rate* *No Security*	Cash Now *Short Term* *Rapid Payments* *High Interest Rate* *Full Security*

FIGURE 5

Sellers want the highest possible price and stringent terms. Buyers, on the other hand, desire the lowest possible price and the most lenient terms. It is necessary to bridge this tension in order to balance the interests of the buyer and seller(s) in possible future transactions. This is why a central theme of this book is to reach agreement at the outset on as many aspects of future transactions as possible.

Many buy-sell agreements which are not funded by life insurance provide for payment over a term of years. We have seen payment terms as short as two or three years, and as long as 10 years. Other agreements call for lump sum payments, often funded by life insurance.

There are many funding structures for buy-sell agreements. The following list will provide an idea of the variety of possibilities and serve as a stimulus for discussion.

- ⊚ **Life insurance.** Some agreements are funded, in whole or in part, by life insurance on the lives of the individual shareholders. When it is available and affordable, life insurance is a tidy solution for funding in the event of death. However, it is important to think through the implications of life insurance.

  The proceeds of a life insurance policy owned by a company naturally flow to the company. A critical question immediately arises: Should the insurance proceeds be added to the value (as a nonoperating asset) before reaching a conclusion of value for the buy-sell agreement? Arguably, the life insurance proceeds could be considered as an asset to be included in the calculation of value for the deceased shareholder's shares. Arguably, as well, the life insurance proceeds could be considered as a separate asset for the purposes of the buy-sell agreement, and not included in the determination of value.

  This is a subject that warrants discussion and agreement while all parties are alive. It is a difficult question to address when one party is dead. Absent specific instructions in the buy-sell agreement, the appraisers may have to decide. What they decide will almost certainly disappoint one or both sides. See the further discussion in Chapter 15.

- ⊚ **Cash.** There are several potential sources of cash for buy-sell redemptions of stock, including the following:

  - **Life insurance.** See the comments above.

  - **Corporate assets.** Depending on the size of the required redemption, there may be sufficient corporate assets which may have been accumulated in excess of operating requirements over time to accomplish the purchase. However, these assets would have to be accumulated during the selling shareholder's ownership period(s) and would likely be included in the valuation.

- **External borrowings.** Depending on the financial condition and outlook for the company, it may be able to borrow sufficient funds from a financial institution to pay the purchase price.

◎ **Selling shareholder notes.** Some buy-sell agreements call for the company to issue a note for the amount of the required stock redemption. If this is the case, the terms of the note should be specified clearly in the agreement. Cash payments are usually preferable to sellers because their risk associated with the buying company is relieved. However, notes are often necessary for companies in order to facilitate orderly transactions.

◎ **Combinations of cash and shareholder notes.** Whether in the form of a down payment or as the first payment on an extended note, many agreements call for a portion of the purchase price to be paid at closing. Once again, it is easier to negotiate these terms at the outset than for either party to have to worry about the financing aspects following a trigger event.

Any time shareholder notes are used to finance a buy sell repurchase, it is necessary to ensure that the transaction does not unreasonably impair the capital of the business. In many states, state law prohibits corporations from engaging in transactions that could impair capital or raise questions of insolvency. Your legal counsel will have to advise you regarding this issue and ensure that the language of your agreement protects the company and selling shareholders to the extent necessary and appropriate.

There are a number of possible structures for notes (or cash-down-plus notes) that might be considered for buy-sell agreement redemptions. Figure 6 provides a starting point for discussion of this important issue.

Absent specific agreement on the funding mechanism, the value of a buy-sell agreement as a vehicle to repurchase shares from departed shareholders may be lessened significantly. Even with a stated funding mechanism, the economic or present value of any redemption price set by the agreement can be significantly reduced because of an inadequate interest rate or excessive risk to be borne by the selling shareholder.

Everyone is familiar with the old saying, "You can name the price if I can name the terms." Weak terms in a funding mechanism diminish the value of the agreement from the viewpoint of future sellers. On the other hand, terms that are too strong can make it difficult for companies to perform in circumstances calling for substantial repurchases.

I hope it is clear by now that it is essential for you and your fellow owners to agree on funding mechanisms when creating buy-sell agreements.

BASIC CONSIDERATIONS FOR SHAREHOLDER NOTES IN BUY-SELL AGREEMENTS

Potential Areas for Agreement	Comment	Company Perspectives	Selling Shareholder Perspectives
Term of Note	Typical terms range from two years on the low side to as many as ten years.	Longer terms tend to be preferable to assure flexibility and ability to pay with least impact on the business.	Shorter terms tend to be preferable in order to complete transaction and eliminate credit exposure to the company.
Form of Note	The form of the note can range from interest-only, to amortizing over the term with equal payments, to equal payments of principal each year (or quarter or month), together with interest.	Interest-only provides the most flexibility to companies and defers payment as long as possible.	Amortizing notes - equal stream of payments Equal payments of principal each period - declining stream of payments Interest-only is riskiest and defers payment of principal to maturity. If credit exposure is not an issue, longer deferral of principal payments extends payment of capital gains with installment sale treatment of the note.
Down Payment	The down payment can range from nothing down, to a set percentage of the total price at closing, to requiring that the first payment of an amortizing note be paid at closing.	Low down payments provide the greatest flexibility to companies.	Larger down payments provide current liquidity for selling shareholders and minimize future risk of credit exposure to the company.

FIGURE 6

BASIC CONSIDERATIONS FOR SHAREHOLDER NOTES IN BUY-SELL AGREEMENTS

Potential Areas for Agreement	Comment	Company Perspectives	Selling Shareholder Perspectives
Payment Schedule	Payment schedules can range from monthly to quarterly to annually.	Monthly payments are generally considered to be too frequent by most companies. Annual payments provide the greatest flexibility.	Sellers often prefer monthly payments for predictability, but will often agree on quarterly payments.
Interest Rate: Level	The interest rate on the loan is an important element and requires careful consideration. The manner in which the interest rate is set should be clearly stated in terms that will be clear in the future.	Companies tend to desire a relatively low interest rate to minimize cash flow requirements.	Sellers need to have a reasonable (market) rate to assure a risk-adjusted return on the note while awaiting repayment of principal. Below market rates reduce the present value of the purchase price.
Interest Rate: Floating or Fixed	Depends on company and shareholder tolerance to interest rate exposure during term of notes. With a floating rate and a regular amortization, the amortization schedule must be recalculated as rates change. If the rate is based on the *Wall Street Journal* prime rate as of, say, the trigger date, the agreement must be clear if the rate is fixed at that level or repriced periodically. Unclear language creates big problems.	Many companies will tend to desire to fix the interest rate to eliminate exposure to rising rates over the term of notes.	Sellers need to consider the risk of interest rate exposure with floating rates relative to the consistency assured by fixed rate notes.

FIGURE 6 (CONTINUED)

BASIC CONSIDERATIONS FOR SHAREHOLDER NOTES IN BUY-SELL AGREEMENTS

Potential Areas for Agreement	Comment	Company Perspectives	Selling Shareholder Perspectives
Priority in Company's Capital Structure	Must specify position in capital structure. If this element is not specified, it will likely assure that shareholder notes are effectively subordinated debt, i.e., subordinated to all other lenders and other creditors.	Companies tend to want notes to be unsecured and at the bottom of the capital structure. A shareholder note without other protections or security is favorable financing and tantamount to subordinated debt.	Many agreements give no thought of subordination to other creditors. If a seller note is effectively subordinated to all other creditors, then the interest rate should reflect its relative risk in relationship to other borrowings. The effect of an inadequate interest rate relative to risk is to devalue the note relative to its par value. Sellers may desire that future incremental financings be subordinated to their notes or else company will need to pre-pay.
Security	The question for consideration is whether the shareholder note will be secured in any fashion by the general assets of the company, by specific assets owned by the company, or by stock in the company.	Companies tend to prefer that shareholder notes not be secured. Having them unsecured provides maximum flexibility for future financings.	Sellers will want to have security for their notes. At the very least, the shares that have been sold can be the security. Since remaining shareholders benefit from the company's purchase of shares under the agreement, a portion of their shares could be held as collateral. Certainly, shareholders desire to be assured that future financings of the company will be subordinated to their debt.

FIGURE 6 (CONTINUED)

BASIC CONSIDERATIONS FOR SHAREHOLDER NOTES IN BUY-SELL AGREEMENTS

Potential Areas for Agreement	Comment	Company Perspectives	Selling Shareholder Perspectives
Prepayment: Right or Obligation	Prepayment can be an issue under a number of circumstances and is one that should be covered in buy-sell agreements.	A company may desire the right to prepay a note to assure flexibility regarding cash flow and future financings. Companies prefer that there be no prepayment penalty.	Prepayment can be beneficial to sellers in that they achieve liquidity earlier than planned. However, if the prepayment terminates a note with an attractive interest rate (relatively high) and the rate cannot be replaced in the markets, prepayment may be unfavorable. Sellers will want mandatory prepayment if the company is sold or engages in a substantial recapitalization that could jeopardize a note's creditworthiness.
Events of Default / Rights of Holder / Ability of Company to Cure	Surprisingly, many buy-sell agreements do not discuss events of default regarding shareholder notes at all.	If events of default, such as the failure to make a payment, are considered, the company will want the right to cure the default within a short period of time.	In the event of default not timely cured, sellers may want the ability to accelerate the note such that it is due in full.
Other Terms per Counsel	As recommended and agreed to by owners and the company.		

FIGURE 6 (CONTINUED)

FOUR EXAMPLES TO AVOID

I've reflected on the many buy-sell agreements I've reviewed in recent years. Let's focus on four that have issues with either what appraisers call the level of value, or with appraiser qualifications. Any facts have been altered to protect the innocent (or guilty) as the case may be.

- **Family business, buy-sell agreement drafted in the early-1980s.** A family member dies and the buy-sell agreement is triggered. Everyone assumes that the valuation called for in the agreement was at the nonmarketable minority level, since the interest involved is about 30%. Upon reading the agreement, it is clear to me that the valuation language calls for an enterprise value, without minority interest or marketability discounts. *The family's estate plan is put in jeopardy.*

- **Family business, buy-sell agreement drafted in the latter-1980s.** This agreement provides the right to "put," or to offer shares to other family members at either an agreed-upon price (which does not exist currently) or based on an appraisal process. There are issues in the appraiser selection process and in the definition of value in this agreement. *The valuation process calling for as many as three appraisers is rendered problematic.*

⊙ **Closely held business, buy-sell agreement drafted in the early 2000s.** The agreement calls for an appraisal of the company, i.e., at an enterprise level, but then leaves to the appraiser the decision of whether any valuation discounts apply to a particular shareholder's interest. There are no agreed-upon qualifications for the appraiser selection process. If a dispute arises, up to two additional appraisers could be used who could also exercise their judgment regarding whether valuation discounts apply. *This is a disaster in waiting.*

⊙ **Closely held business, recent vintage.** This agreement is sensitive to defining an enterprise value in the valuation process, but has later language that raises questions about this conclusion. With no qualifications established for the appraiser selection process, any valuation process is at considerable risk regarding the selection of the appraiser(s). *Confused or confusing language results in major confusion in the valuation process.*

My challenge to you is to eliminate obvious problems with your buy-sell agreement that can be easily avoided with regard to selection of an appraiser.

Chapter Fourteen

The Defining Elements of a Valuation Process Agreement Explained

I often use the term "words on the page." Appraisers retained pursuant to the operation of buy-sell agreements are normally bound to prepare their valuations in accordance with the kind of value described or defined within the agreements. In other words, the "words on the page" will determine the kind of value to be developed in the appraisal. Collectively, these criteria become the assignment definition.

Previously, we introduced the five defining elements of a valuation process agreement, as well as another critical element, the funding mechanism.

1. Standard of Value	4. Qualifications of Appraisers
2. Level of Value	5. Appraisal Standards
3. The "As Of" Date	6. Funding Mechanisms

In this chapter, we will focus on the five elements that are necessary to define the valuation assignment in your valuation process agreement. In Chapter 15, we will further discuss the funding mechanism, and, in particular, the treatment of life insurance associated with buy-sell agreements.

Defining Element #1:
The Standard of Value

The first defining element is the *standard of value* that must be specified in the engagement.

The word "value" has many meanings. Value, like beauty, may lie in the eye of the beholder. That there is some confusion about what is meant by value is confirmed by legal scholar James C. Bonbright, who stated:

> As long as common law and statute law persist in using the "value" as a legal jack-of-all-trades, judges are forced, willy-nilly, to reject the precedent of economists and instead to follow the precedent of Humpty Dumpty (from *Through a Looking Glass*): "When I use a word, it means what I choose it to mean – neither more nor less."[4]

If the words on the pages are not clear regarding the standard of value, appraisers may be placed in the position of Humpty Dumpty, and have to decide what the words on the page mean. When agreements are silent or unclear as to the standard of value, the appraiser(s) may have to make decisions they would prefer not to make. Otherwise, the parties, whose interests have already diverged, will have to decide on the standard of value to provide instructions to the appraiser(s). Neither situation is ideal.

Fair Market Value

The most common standard of value is that of "fair market value." This standard applies to virtually all federal and estate tax valuation matters, including charitable gifts, gift or estate tax issues, ad valorem taxes, and other tax-related issues. Fair market value is also the applicable standard of value in many bankruptcy cases involving valuation issues.

---

4   Bonbright, James C., *Valuation of Property* (1937), as quoted in George D. McCarthy and Robert E. Healy, *Valuing a Company: Practices and Procedures* (New York: Ronald Press, 1971), p. 3.

Fair market value has been defined in many court cases. It is also defined in Internal Revenue Service Revenue Ruling 59-60 as:

> ....the price at which a property would change hands between a willing buyer and a willing seller when the former is not under any compulsion to buy and the latter is not under any compulsion to sell, both parties having reasonable knowledge of relevant facts. Court decisions frequently state in addition that the hypothetical buyer and seller are assumed to be able, as well as willing, to trade and to be well-informed about the property and concerning the market for such property. (Internal Revenue Bulletin 1959-1 CB 237, IRC Sec. 2031)

Fair market value is similarly defined in the Glossary of the *ASA Business Valuation Standards of the American Society of Appraisers* as:

> The price, expressed in cash equivalents, at which property would change hands between a hypothetical willing and able buyer and a hypothetical willing and able seller, acting at arm's length in an open and unrestricted market, when neither is under compulsion to buy or sell and when both have reasonable knowledge of the relevant facts. (Note: In Canada, the term "price" should be replaced with the term "highest price.")

Fair market value is an arm's length standard that assumes there are willing and informed buyers and sellers, neither buyers nor sellers are acting under any compulsion, and both buyers and sellers have the financial capacity to engage in transactions. In other words, the parties are assumed to have independent interests and act on their own behalf. That's why it is called an arm's length standard.

Revenue Ruling 59-60 suggests that "all available financial data, as well as all relevant factors affecting fair market value, should be considered." Eight specific factors are listed in Revenue Ruling 59-60 as fundamental and the subject of required analysis in fair market value determinations. I call these factors the *Basic Eight* factors of valuation:

1. The nature of the business and the history of the enterprise from its inception

2. The economic outlook in general and the condition and outlook of the specific industry in particular

3. The book value of the stock and the financial condition of the business

4. The earning capacity of the company

5. The dividend-paying capacity

6. Whether or not the enterprise has goodwill or other intangible value

7. Sales of the stock and the size of the block to be valued

8. The market price of stocks for corporations that are engaged in the same or a similar line of business and that have their stocks traded in a free and open market, either on an exchange or over-the-counter

In any consideration of the *Basic Eight* factors, there is considerable room for the exercise of judgment. Just prior to discussing these factors for analysis, Revenue Ruling 59-60 states that "A sound valuation will be based upon all the relevant facts, but the *elements of common sense, informed judgment and reasonableness* must enter into the process of weighing those facts and weighing their significance." (*emphasis* added)

The emphasized elements – common sense, informed judgment, and reasonableness – are critical in fair market value determinations.

Fair market value is the standard of value specified in many, probably most, buy-sell agreements. It is, therefore, important that business owners, attorneys, and other advisors have a working knowledge of this standard.

Other Standards of Value

There are a number of other standards of value, including "fair value" and "investment value." Fair value is, on the one hand, a statutory concept. Fair value is the standard of value in most states in dissenting minority shareholder and shareholder oppression matters. The standard is seldom defined in state statutes, and is interpreted by the courts of various states. Needless to say, the application of the fair value concept in a buy-sell agreement needlessly introduces potentially confusing state law into the definition of fair value. I do not recommend the use of this concept, even though you might think it is, well, "fair."

If statutory fair value weren't potentially confusing enough, another concept of fair value has emerged in the accounting arena. The term "fair value" is associated with financial statement reporting per ASC Topic 820, *Fair Value Measurements and Disclosures*. ASC 820 (formerly SFAS 157) defines fair value for financial reporting purposes, establishes a framework to measure fair value under GAAP, and expands disclosures on fair value measurements.

So, in the absence of guidance in an agreement specifying the meaning of fair value, it is possible that an appraiser, particularly an appraiser with an accounting background, could look to guidance in the evolving accounting literature for assistance.

The bottom line for fair value as a standard of value for buy-sell agreements is that you may be in for surprises as to what fair value means and you may end up thinking that the result you get is anything but "fair."

Other standards of value sometimes appear in buy-sell agreements. If the standard of value is not clearly defined, the result is ambiguity and uncertainty.

Appraisers may disagree in their interpretations, or they may have to request interpretations from parties whose interests are now adverse. Consider the following "standards" of value from actual buy-sell agreements:

- **"Provide a valuation on a going-concern basis."** This description suggests that the appraisal be provided assuming that the subject enterprise will continue as a going concern. However, there is ambiguity as to the particular level of value that should be applicable, and appraisers could legitimately exercise different judgments in interpreting its meaning.

- **"Investment value."** Investment value is typically described as value from the perspective of a particular buyer. But which buyer? Appraisers will not know unless there is more complete specification of the kind of value desired by the parties. Differing interpretations can lead to disparate valuation conclusions between appraisers.

- **"The value."** Agreements calling for "the value" of the shares or, for example, "the current value" of the shares are not helpful. Such language is nonspecific and subject to wide ranging interpretations.

Recall the quote from Humpty Dumpty at the beginning of this chapter.

Conclusion on the Standard of Value

The standard of value must be clearly stated. If there is ambiguity in the definition or terms used to describe the particular kind of value to which the parties of a buy-sell agreement have agreed, the probability for problems, disagreements, and potential litigation rises to unacceptable levels.

If you choose the fair market value standard of value, I recommend that your agreement cite the definition from the *ASA Business Valuation Standards* in your agreement. Citing (or quoting) this definition ensures clarity regarding the standard of value and references accepted business valuation standards. In the alternative, you can cite and/or quote the definition from Revenue Ruling 59-60.

In the absence of a compelling reason to use another standard of value, I generally recommend fair market value as the standard of value for buy-sell agreements.

Defining Element #2: The Level of Value

What is a level of value and why is it important? These are two of the most important questions facing drafters of buy-sell agreements.

There is no such thing as "the value" of a closely held business. Confusion over an appraiser's basis of value, either by appraisers or by users of appraisal reports, can lead to the placing of inappropriately high or low values for a buy-sell agreement transaction. Therefore, it is essential that both business appraisers and the parties using appraisals be aware of the correct basis (level) of value. Then, appropriate valuation methodologies can be applied in deriving the conclusion of value for any interest being appraised.

The levels of value chart is an economic and financial model used by appraisers to describe the complexities of behavior of individuals and businesses in the process of buying and selling businesses and business interests. It attempts to cut through the detailed maze of facts that give rise to individual transactions involving particular business interests. The model generally describes the valuation relationships that emerge from observing many thousands of individual transactions.

It is understandable if you are confused over the various levels of value. Business owners tend to think of value in terms of an "enterprise" basis or perhaps a "sale" basis. Valuation professionals look more at terminology like "controlling interest" basis or "minority interest" basis.

Levels of Value Charts

The levels of value chart has been around for many years. The original chart showed three levels, as indicated in Figure 7.

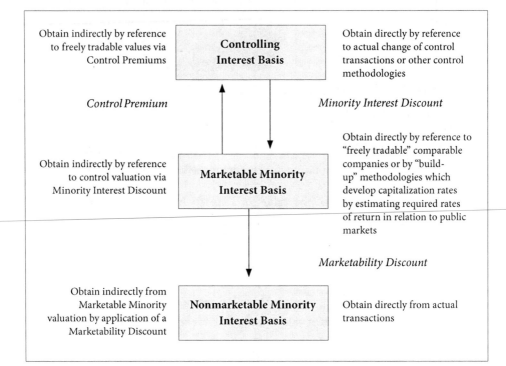

FIGURE 7

In current thinking, there are four conceptual levels of value.

⊙ **Strategic control value** refers to the value of an enterprise as a whole, incorporating the strategic intent that may motivate particular buyers and the expected business and financial synergies that may result from its acquisition. Higher expected cash flows relative to financial buyers may enable strategic (or synergistic) purchasers to pay premiums, often called strategic control premiums, relative to financial control values. A strategic buyer may also

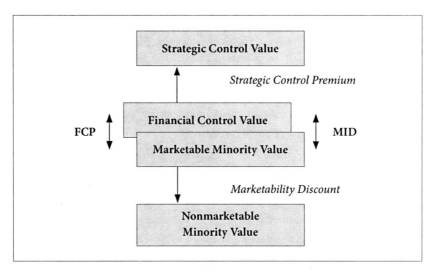

FIGURE 8

increase the price it will pay based on the use of its own, presumably lower, cost of capital.

⊚ **Financial control value** refers to the value of an enterprise, excluding any synergies that may accrue to a strategic buyer. This level of value is viewed from the perspective of a financial buyer, who may expect to benefit from improving the enterprise's cash flow but not through any synergies that may be available to a strategic buyer.

• Many business appraisers believe that the marketable minority and the financial control levels of value are, if not synonymous, then essentially the same.

One way of describing the financial control value is that buyers are willing to pay for the expected cash flows of enterprises and will pay no more than the marketable minority value. However, they may believe they can run a company better *and* if the competitive bidding situation requires that they share a portion of potential improvements with the seller, these two levels can diverge somewhat.

- **FCP** is the *financial control premium.* The financial control premium is shown, conceptually, to be nil, or at least very small in Figure 8.

- **MID** is the *minority interest discount.* The minority interest discount is also shown to be conceptually nil or very small. This is consistent with the discount being the conceptual inverse of the financial control premium, which is itself nil or very small.

Recently, with the large influx of capital into private equity groups and hedge funds, competitive pressure for deals has caused some financial buyers to compete with strategic buyers. To do so, they must lower their expected rates of return, since strategic or synergistic cash flow benefits are not generally available to them.

Appraisers look in part to the transaction markets for pricing guidelines when developing valuation at the strategic and financial control levels of value.

- **Marketable minority value** refers to the value of a minority interest, lacking control, but enjoying the benefit of liquidity as if it were freely tradable in an active market. This level of value is also described as the "as-if-freely-traded" level of value.

Minority investors in actively traded public companies cannot exercise control over companies. However, they can exercise control over whether they hold shares or sell them. In selling, they obtain the current share price, which is their pro rata share of the public market's pricing of the companies.

Appraisers look to similar publicly traded companies, in part, to develop valuations at the marketable minority level of value.

⊙ **Nonmarketable minority value** refers to the value of a minority interest, lacking both control and market liquidity. Value at this level is determined based on the expected future enterprise cash flows that are available to minority shareholders, discounted to the present at an appropriate discount rate over the expected holding period of the investment. The nonmarketable minority level of value is derived indirectly by applying a marketability discount directly to marketable minority indications of value, or directly, by determining the present value of expected cash flows to minority interests.

All charts, as well as the underlying valuation theory, can also be found in the book *Business Valuation: An Integrated Theory of Business Valuation Second Edition* (John Wiley & Sons, Inc., 2007), which I wrote with co-author Travis W. Harms, CFA, CPA/ABV.

The selection of the level of value, in conjunction with the standard of value, begins to specify a valuation or appraisal assignment of a particular business or business interest. Without looking at any numbers, it is clear that the strategic control level of value is higher (more valuable on a per-share or pro rata basis) than is the nonmarketable minority level of value.

In any multiple appraiser valuation process, if one appraiser believes that the appropriate level of value is strategic control and the other believes that the nonmarketable minority level of value is appropriate, the disparity in their conclusions will be wide. That is why business owners have to agree on these two important elements that help to specify the appraisals that will be performed based on their buy-sell agreements.

Practical Thoughts on the Levels of Value

You may ask, how can there be any confusion about the appropriate level of value in a buy-sell agreement? Isn't everyone familiar with these valuation concepts? The answer is "no." Where there is a lack of understanding about valuation concepts, confusion will reign.

Recall the old expression: "A picture is worth a thousand words." Here's a word picture and then a visual picture.

The Word Picture

Assume that a buy-sell agreement was triggered and the company was required to acquire a shareholder's shares per its terms. Unfortunately, the agreement had vague and confusing language regarding the level of value.

The company retained a well-qualified business appraiser, as did the shareholder. Under the terms of the agreement, each was required to provide a valuation.

- The company's appraiser interpreted the level of value as the *nonmarketable minority* level of value, citing specific language in the agreement to support her conclusion. In developing her opinion, she concluded that the financial control/marketable minority level of value was $100 per share. A marketability discount of 40% was applied and the interest was valued at $60 per share.

- The shareholder's appraiser interpreted the level of value as the *strategic control* level of value, citing specific language in the agreement in support of his conclusion. He also concluded that the financial control/marketable minority level of value was $100 per share. A control premium of 40% was applied and the interest was valued at $140 per share.

The Visual Picture

The conclusions of value at each level of value are shown in Figure 9. Note that there is exact agreement on value at the financial control/marketable minority level. Further note the dramatic difference in concluded values after reaching their respective final values – $60 per share versus $140 per share.

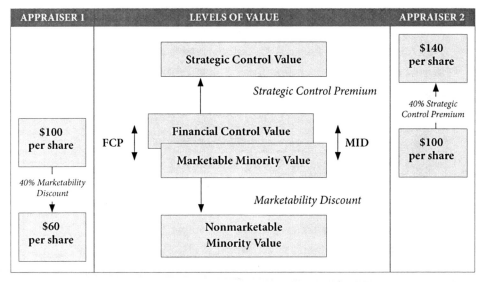

FIGURE 9

The parties now have two appraisals. They are quite similar in many respects, but widely different in their conclusions of value. The visual picture raises several questions for consideration:

- How could this have happened?

- How will the mandatory third appraiser reconcile the (irreconcilable) differences in concluded values?

- Could this happen to you? The fact that this sort of thing does happen is one of the reasons I have written this book. I hope you find that it helps you and your fellow owners to avoid making the same mistakes. The example, by the way, is based on an actual situation where I was the third appraiser. Situations like this can and do happen, and they are never pretty in their resolution, nor are the parties satisfied with the ultimate results.

Suggestions for Specifying the Desired Level of Value

We observed that the financial control/marketable minority level of value may work for many agreements. Beyond that, I make no recommendation regarding which level of value is appropriate for purposes of your agreement, but suggest the following:

- Reach agreement on which level of value is desired for your agreement and specify that level of value in your agreement by specific reference to a levels of value chart.
- Refer to a chart in this book in your agreement to eliminate any questions that appraisers who might be retained at future trigger events might have.

If you follow this advice, you should get the kind of valuation you and your fellow owners agreed on. You can ensure this by adopting the *Single Appraiser, Select Now and Value Now* process described in Chapter 17.

Defining Element #3: The "As Of" Date of the Appraisal

This chapter addresses the concept of the "as of" or the "effective date" or the "valuation date." The issue of the "as of" date is far more important than the brevity of this section might otherwise indicate.

The "as of" date is required to be defined for an appraisal under prevailing business valuation standards. Four terms are used interchangeably in these standards to peg the date as of which a valuation will be rendered:

"effective date," "valuation date," an "appraisal date," and the "as of" date. We, nevertheless, use the term "as of" date to focus attention on the specific point in time as of which the appraiser's opinion of value applies.

The "as of" date is the date as of which available information pertaining to a valuation should be considered by appraisers. The effective date grounds the appraiser not only in the background and financial condition of a subject company, but also in its local, regional, or national economy, as well as its industry and other relevant aspects.

The "As Of" Date Determines Information

We know from the definition of fair market value that both parties to a transaction are assumed to have reasonable knowledge about an investment and the relevant facts pertaining to it. *This knowledge is grounded in the "as of" date.*

Real-life transactions are based on facts and circumstances known up to the minute of their closings and are considered reasonable outlooks for the future. Making reasonably or fully informed choices does not mean having a crystal ball that eliminates uncertainties by forecasting the future with precision.

Appraisers engaging in *after-the-fact* valuations should not abuse the standard of reasonable knowledge based on facts that clarified themselves shortly or long after an historical valuation date. Attorneys representing parties in a dispute that benefit from knowledge of post-valuation date events may want to believe that the certainty of those events was reasonably knowable at the valuation date. And parties to a buy-sell agreement may want to believe similarly depending on their perspective with respect to a contemplated transaction. Independent appraisers do not have this luxury.

In some instances, the fact that an event *might* occur in the future is known at the time of the valuation date. What is not generally known is *when* or with *what probability* the event might occur. Appraisers must assess those probabilities and incorporate the risks or potential benefits appropriately in their appraisals. They must consider what willing and reasonably informed hypothetical investors might do based on information available as of a valuation date.

It is critical that the "as of" date be specified. It may also be important to determine what happens in the event of delays in the appraisal process. Otherwise, one or both parties may be at risk to changes in the company or its industry over time.

Defining Element #4: Appraiser Qualifications

Buy-sell agreements are often silent regarding appraiser qualifications.

Several aspects of appraiser qualifications should be considered. As stated earlier, we believe it can be beneficial for the parties to go through an appraisal selection process at the outset of agreements. The logical requirements become fairly apparent as parties begin to consider individual appraisers and appraisal firms. Danger, in the form of future angst and uncertainty, arises for the operation of agreements when qualifications are not specified.

Qualifications of Appraisal Firms

When selecting an appraisal firm, it is desirable that the firm (or, at least, its legitimate successor) will be around when future trigger events occur. It may be a good idea to describe the qualifications of appraisal firms in the context of their size and longevity, as well as the scope of their business.

Qualifications of Appraisers

Appraisal firms do not render appraisal reports – appraisers do. Therefore, it is also important to consider the qualifications of the individual appraisers. Evaluation of the qualifications of business appraisers can include consideration of a number of distinguishing factors, including:

- **Education.** Business appraisers typically have college degrees in fields like finance, economics, accounting, and mathematics, among others. Many appraisers also have advanced degrees.

- **Valuation training.** The various appraisal societies, including the American Society of Appraisers (ASA), the American Institute of Certified Public Accountants (AICPA), the Institute of Business Appraisers (IBA), the National Association of Certified Valuation Analysts (NACVA), and the Canadian Institute of Chartered Business Valuators (CICBV) provide business valuation courses as part of their ongoing education and credentialing processes.

- **Appraisal experience.** You may want to specify the level of experience necessary to qualify an appraiser for your buy-sell agreement. However, all experience is not equal. While two appraisers may have the same number of years of experience, one may have had 10 years of continuing growth as a professional, while the other may have had the same tenure of experience repeated 10 times. Appraisers with mid-sized and larger firms are likely to have good experience because of the nature of their businesses. There are also many qualified experienced appraisers in smaller firms and practices. You will not be able to make a judgment without some personal investigation.

- **Industry experience.** Sometimes, specific industry experience is noted as a requirement. This is a potentially dangerous qualification since industry experience is not equivalent to valuation experience and training.

  - Many companies are in narrow industry niches that are simply too small for appraisers to develop specialty niches.

- Many industries, even small ones, do have niche brokers who work primarily to sell companies in their niches.

- While it can be tempting to think that brokerage-related "industry experience" is important, unless it is combined with actual independent appraisal experience, it will not be helpful.

- Further, many industry brokers tend to focus on strategic values only and may not be familiar with other relevant valuation considerations.

⊚ **Continuing education.** There are numerous sources for ongoing study in the business valuation field. The appraisal societies and other groups provide CPE credit in a variety of local, regional, and national seminars and conventions. Some valuation firms provide specific valuation training for their professionals on a regular basis. Others send their professionals to seminars or have them attend webinars or other educational offerings. The various appraisal societies require continuing education ranging from 12 hours per year (IBA) to 40 hours per year (AICPA).

⊚ **Publishing.** Individual appraisers may demonstrate their knowledge, training, and experience by writing about business and valuation issues. Some appraisers have written books, and many have written articles for professional and business publications.

⊚ **Credentialing.** A number of professional designations are offered by the professional appraisal associations. Details about the various credentials can be found on the web sites of the respective associations. Holding a business valuation credential from one of these organizations is one indication of commitment to the business valuation profession. Some appraisers hold multiple designations.

APPRAISAL ORGANIZATIONS
AND PROFESSIONAL CREDENTIALS

American Society of Appraisers (ASA)

- ⊚ The ASA offers the AM (Accredited Member), the ASA (Accredited Senior Appraiser) and the FASA (Fellow of the American Society of Appraisers) designations.

- ⊚ The ASA also offers a credential (also called ASA) in Appraisal Review.

- ⊚ www.appraisers.org

American Institute of Certified Public Accountants (AICPA)

- ⊚ The AICPA offers the ABV (Accredited in Business Valuation) credential.

- ⊚ bvfls.aicpa.org

Institute of Business Appraisers (IBA)

- ⊚ The IBA offers the CBA (Certified in Business Appraisal) designation.

- ⊚ The IBA also offers the ABAR (Accredited in Business Appraisal Review) designation.

- ⊚ www.go-iba.org

National Association of Certified Valuation Analysts (NACVA)

- ⊚ The NACVA offers the CVA (Certified Valuation Analyst) and the AVA (Accredited Valuation Analyst) designations.

- ⊚ www.nacva.com

Canadian Institute of Chartered Business Valuators (CICBV)

- ⊚ The CICBV offers the CBV (Chartered Business Valuator) designation.

- ⊚ www.cicbv.ca

CFA Institute

- ⊚ The CFA Institute offers the CFA (Chartered Financial Analyst) designation.

- ⊚ www.cfainstitute.org

- ⊚ **Expert testimony experience.** Hopefully, there will be no need for expert testimony regarding your buy-sell agreement. However, acceptance by courts as an expert witness in adversarial proceedings does represent another aspect of independent review of qualifications. If your buy-sell agreement gives rise to litigation, you will definitely desire that your expert have expert testimony experience.

- ⊚ **Required compliance with professional standards.** Individuals who are accredited by the above organizations are required to follow codes of ethics and professional standards promulgated by their respective organizations. Members of the American of Society of Appraisers must also follow the *Uniform Standards of Professional Appraisal Practice* promulgated by the Appraisal Foundation, as well as the *ASA Business Valuation Standards* of the American Society of Appraisers. Members of the AICPA must follow *Statement on Standards for Valuation Services No. 1.* Appraisers who are members of other organizations must follow their respective standards. Further, appraisers can comply with specific standards voluntarily.

⊚ **Speaking.** Individual appraisers may also demonstrate their knowledge, training, and experience by speaking to professional and business organizations. As with publishing, speaking is a form of educating one's peers, fellow professionals in related fields, and business owners.

Selecting Appraisers

An excellent way to avoid uncertainty regarding the future selection of appraisers is to decide on the appraiser(s) prior to the signing of the buy-sell agreement. A further aspect of this recommendation is that the selected appraiser can provide an initial appraisal under the agreed upon standard of value at the agreed upon level of value. Further, the firm employing the selected appraiser may have other qualified appraisers who can carry out necessary future assignments in the event the named appraiser is not available.

Using this chapter as a guide, the parties could decide on the specific minimum qualifications for any future appraiser selection under the buy-sell agreement. One such qualification might be, for example, that the selected appraiser holds the Accredited Senior Appraiser (ASA) designation from the American Society of Appraisers. This would ensure that the selected appraiser was credentialed and had a minimum of five years of full time experience in business appraisal, and likely much more.

If you select accreditation by the American Society of Appraisers as one qualification, you are assured that their appraisers' reports must comply with the *ASA Business Valuation Standards*, the *Principles of Appraisal Practice and Code of Ethics* of the American Society of Appraisers and the *Uniform Standards of Professional Appraisal Practice* promulgated by the Appraisal Foundation.

If you select accreditation by the AICPA as one qualification, you are assured that their appraisers' reports must comply with *Statement on Standards for Valuation Services No. 1.*

While such specification may seem unnecessary, it is far better to have the discussions now. If each side will obtain a business appraiser, then it is critical that they have similar experience levels and operate under the same business valuation standards.

My bottom line regarding appraiser selection is that it is far better to make the choice(s) before there is a trigger event and to document the choice(s) in the agreement.

Defining Element #5: Appraisal Standards

Professions are defined by the existence of requirements for entrance into them, as well as by professional standards that govern the minimum requirements of operation and conduct.

Business appraisers who are credentialed by the appraisal and educational organizations are required to operate their appraisal practices in accordance with standards of professional practice and codes of ethics. Standards are very important to the future success of your buy-sell agreement appraisal processes.

There are several sets of business appraisal standards. Information regarding each organization's standards can be found on their respective web sites (see previous discussion).

- **Uniform Standards of Professional Appraisal Practice (USPAP).** Promulgated by the Appraisal Standards Board of The Appraisal Foundation, USPAP, as the standards are known, was developed originally in 1986-87. USPAP has been adopted by major appraisal organizations in North America, and "represents the generally accepted and recognized standards of appraisal practice in the United States." Standards Rules 3 of USPAP relates to appraisal review. Standards Rules 9 and 10 relate to the conduct and reporting of business appraisal reports. These standards are updated every two years.

◎ **ASA Business Valuation Standards.** The Business Valuation Committee of the American Society of Appraisers develops and maintains these standards. Development began in 1990, and the first standards were published in 1992. They have been expanded and updated, and they are updated periodically.

- **Principles of Appraisal Practice and Code of Ethics.** This document is published by the American Society of Appraisers and is applicable to all members of the Society, including members in the business valuation discipline.

◎ **AICPA Statement on Standards for Valuation Services (SSVS) No. 1.** The AICPA has published these standards as guidance for CPAs who provide business valuation services.

◎ **Institute of Business Appraisers Business Valuation Standards** and **Rules of Professional Conduct.** The Institute of Business Appraisers advances standards and rules of professional conduct for its members.

◎ **NACVA Professional Standards.** The National Association of Certified Valuation Analysts publishes these professional standards applicable to its members.

◎ **CFA Institute Code of Ethics & Standards of Professional Conduct.** The CFA Institute advances these standards as the "ethical cornerstone" of the organization. Although the CFA designation is not specifically a business valuation credential, a growing number of business appraisers are earning the designation.

The set(s) of appraisal standards to be followed in valuations for buy-sell agreements is a defining element from a valuation perspective. We state this because there is little chance that appraisers providing valuations pursuant to an agreement will achieve similar results if both are not subject to the same or similar sets of valuation standards and codes of ethics.   Readers are referred to the various websites of the appraisal organizations to obtain their respective standards materials.

Why Standards Should Be Specified

The specification of the standards to be followed is an essential requirement for defining the appraisal mechanism for buy-sell agreements. If the standards are not specified, there is no requirement for individuals selected as appraisers who are not members of one of the national appraisal organizations to follow any set of standards or code of ethics.

A failure to follow generally accepted business valuation standards when conducting appraisals for purposes of buy-sell agreements can foster advocacy on the part of persons selected to perform appraisals. Advocacy clearly undermines the buy-sell agreement appraisal process. Even if such persons maintain their independence throughout an appraisal process, there can easily be the perception of advocacy on the part of one or both parties, which also undermines the process.

Appraisers following USPAP and other standards are required to make a number of very important certifications in each written appraisal. These certifications are designed to assure quality, completeness, and the absence of bias. They also include statements of independence and conformity with the relevant standards.

Conclusion

The first five elements of the appraisal for buy-sell agreements are highlighted.

1. Standard of Value	4. Qualifications of Appraisers
2. Level of Value	5. Appraisal Standards
3. The "As Of" Date	6. Funding Mechanisms

Quoting from the Preamble to USPAP:

> The purpose of the *Uniform Standards of Professional Appraisal Practice (USPAP)* is to promote and maintain a high level of public trust in appraisal practice by establishing requirements for appraisers. It is essential that appraisers develop and communicate their analyses, opinions, and conclusions to intended users of services in a manner that is meaningful and not misleading.

The purpose of appraisal mechanisms in buy-sell agreements should be to specify appraisal processes that will provide *reasonable, consistent, and believable* valuation results. Remember, when buy-sell agreements are signed, no one knows who will be selling and who will be buying. Many buy-sell agreements call for the company to purchase interests of selling shareholders. When this happens, the rest of the shareholders are, in effect, the buyers since they benefit from pro rata increases in their ownership positions.

The appraisal process is critical to the operation of process buy-sell agreements and should be discussed thoughtfully and developed with care so that the parties understand what will happen when trigger events occur. When the business agreements are clearly understood, counsel can then translate them into effective legal language in buy-sell agreements.

DEATH IS THE LEAST LIKELY TRIGGER EVENT

Attorney Peter Osman, in an article for the *Green Bay Press Gazette*, starts off by stating that most businesses have buy-sell agreements. He goes on to say:

> Owners generally draft these agreements because they want to control the transfer of ownership should one of them die or become disabled. Many agreements are set up so that life insurance (or disability insurance) will fund the purchase of the deceased or disabled owner's interest if one of these events occurs.

> Typical buy-sell agreements also contain provisions governing lifetime transfers of ownership, such as divorce, bankruptcy, or retirement of a shareholder, often in the form of a first right of refusal, at a predetermined price in the event one owner wishes to transfer ownership to anyone.

> *Few owners give much thought or analysis to the likelihood of a lifetime transfer of the business. Instead they focus all of their attention on dealing with the least likely event, an owner's death.* For that reason, owners often create buy-sell agreements that work well in the event of a shareholder's death, but fail to realize that the same provisions will govern in the case of a lifetime transfer. Yet, in my experience, lifetime transfers occur much more frequently and, when they do, often cause huge problems. *Because these agreements are designed for one event and used for another, the result can be a disaster for everyone involved.* (*emphasis* added)

Mr. Osman concludes his article with the following advice, which echoes that of this book:

> The best way to prevent this impasse with your company is to address, right now, potential problems caused by a buy-sell agreement drafted years ago for a transfer event that is not the event most likely to occur.

My challenge to you is to recognize that your buy-sell agreement won't meet all the needs of life and death of shareholders unless you and the other owners work on it together and reach agreement.

Chapter Fifteen

Treatment of Life Insurance Proceeds in Valuation

Pete:	**"Does the company own any life insurance policies on the lives of the owners?"**
Sam:	"Well, George and I got policies back when William and Don joined us. Let's see. The value of the company we set was $4 million, so we got policies for $2 million each."
Pete:	**"That was a long time ago. Have you revisited the life insurance question since then?"**
Sam:	"We talked about it when William and Don became owners. I think we reset the value to $6 million at that time. But we never got around to doing anything about it."
Pete:	**"Let's see. The company has policies on you and George for $2 million each and your interests are likely worth about $7 or $8 million each. And William and Don, with 10% of the stock each, have interests worth close to $2 million each."**
Sam:	"Wow! It looks like we really need to look into the life insurance question again."

Pete:	"Does your buy-sell agreement mention what happens to life insurance proceeds in the event someone dies?"
Sam:	"No. I've been through it a couple of times since we've been talking. Not a word."
Pete:	"Let me tell you a story about Harry and Charles."

The overview of funding mechanisms in Chapter 13 indicated that there are two opposing treatments of life insurance proceeds in valuations for purposes of buy-sell agreements.

⊚ **Treatment 1 – Proceeds are a funding vehicle and not a corporate asset.** One treatment would not consider the life insurance proceeds as a corporate asset for valuation purposes. This treatment would recognize that life insurance was purchased on the lives of shareholders for the specific purpose of funding a buy-sell agreement. Under this treatment, life insurance proceeds, if considered as an asset in valuation, would be offset by the company's liability to fund the purchase of shares. Logically, under this treatment, the expense of life insurance premiums on a deceased shareholder would be added back into income as a nonrecurring expense.

⊚ **Treatment 2 – Proceeds are a corporate asset.** Another treatment would consider the life insurance proceeds as a corporate asset for valuation purposes. In the valuation, the proceeds would be treated as a nonoperating asset of the company. This asset, together with all other net assets of the business, would be available to fund the purchase of shares of a deceased shareholder. Again, under this treatment, the expense of life insurance premiums on a deceased shareholder would be added back into income as a nonrecurring expense.

The treatment type selected can have a significant, if not dramatic, effect on the resulting position of a company or a selling shareholder following receipt of life insurance proceeds. It can also affect the company's ability to repurchase the stock of a deceased shareholder. The choice of treatment can also impact the resulting position of any remaining shareholders. Consider the following situation:

- Harry and Charles own 50% interests of High Point Software, and have been partners for many years.

- The buy-sell agreement states that the company will purchase the shares of stock owned by either Harry or Charles in the event of the death of either. The agreement is silent with respect to the treatment of life insurance proceeds and calls for the company to be appraised by me. This may be wishful thinking, perhaps, but this example is based on a true story.

- The company owns term life insurance policies on the lives of Harry and Charles in the amount of $6 million each. Assume for simplicity that there are no corporate income taxes due, or that this figure is net of income taxes.

- Now assume Harry is killed in an accident. Further assume that the company is worth $10 million based on my appraisal prior to consideration of the proceeds of term life insurance owned by the company on the lives of Harry and Charles. Earnings have been normalized in the valuation to adjust for the expense of the term policies.

- Before finalizing the appraisal, I carefully review the buy-sell agreement for direction on the treatment of life insurance proceeds. It is silent on the issue. I call a meeting of Charles and the executor of Harry's estate to discuss the issue, because I know the choice of treatment will make a significant difference to Harry's estate, the company, and to Charles personally as the remaining shareholder.

The valuation impact of each treatment is developed below in the context of the High Point Software example.

Treatment 1: Proceeds Are a Funding Vehicle

Figure 10 summarizes the pre- and post-life insurance values and positions for High Point Software, Harry's estate, and Charles if life insurance proceeds are not considered as a corporate asset in valuation. Note that we are making no assumption about any decrement in value related to the loss of a 50% partner in the business.

PROCEEDS ARE NOT A CORPORATE ASSET

		Company	Harry (Estate)	Charles
1	Stock Ownership (Shares)	100.0	50.0	50.0
2	Stock Ownership (%)	100.0%	50.0%	50.0%
3	Pre- and Post-Life Insurance Value ($m)	$10,000.00	$5,000.00	$5,000.00
4	Life Insurance Proceeds	$6,000.00		
5	Repurchase Liability	($5,000.00)		
6	Post-Life Insurance Value	$11,000.00		
7	Repurchase Stock	($5,000.00)	$5,000.00	
8	Retire / Give Up Stock	(50.0)	(50.0)	
9	Remaining Stock	50.0	0.0	50.0
10	New Stock Ownership (%)	100.0%	0.0%	100.0%
11	Post-Life Insurance Value of Co.	$11,000.00	$0.00	$11,000.00
12	Post-Life Insurance Proceeds		$5,000.00	
13	Net Change in Value from Repurchase	$1,000.00		

FIGURE 10

On Line 3, we see that High Point Software is worth $10 million before consideration of life insurance, and both Harry and Charles have 50% of this value, or $5 million each. Upon Harry's death, the company receives

$6 million of life insurance and recognizes the liability of $5 million to repurchase Harry's stock. The post-life insurance value is $11 million (Lines 4-6). Lines 7-10 reflect the repurchase and retirement of Harry's shares. The remaining company value, after repurchasing Harry's shares for $5 million, is $11 million. Since Charles owns all 50 shares now outstanding, his post-transaction value is $11 million. Harry's estate has received the $5 million of life insurance proceeds from the sale of 50 shares for $5 million.

Treatment 2:
Proceeds Are a Corporate Asset

Figure 11 summarizes the pre- and post-life insurance values and positions for High Point Software, Harry's estate, and Charles if life insurance proceeds are considered as a corporate asset in valuation.

PROCEEDS ARE A CORPORATE ASSET

		Company	Harry (Estate)	Charles
1	Stock Ownership (Shares)	100.0	50.0	50.0
2	Stock Ownership (%)	100.0%	50.0%	50.0%
3	Pre-Life Insurance Value ($m)	$10,000.00	$5,000.00	$5,000.00
4	Life Insurance Proceeds ($m)	$6,000.00	$3,000.00	$3,000.00
5	Post-Life Insurance Value ($m)	$16,000.00	$8,000.00	$8,000.00
6	Repurchase Liability	($8,000.00)		
7	Post-Life Insurance Value	$8,000.00		
8	Repurchase Stock	($8,000.00)	$8,000.00	
9	Retire / Give Up Stock	(50.0)	(50.0)	
10	Remaining Stock	50.0	0.0	50.0
11	New Stock Ownership (%)	100.0%	0.0%	100.0%
12	Post-Life Insurance Value of Co.	$8,000.00	$0.00	$8,000.00
13	Post-Life Insurance Proceeds		$8,000.00	
14	Net Change in Value from Repurchase	($2,000.00)		

FIGURE 11

Line 3 shows the same pre-life insurance value of $10 million as in the treatment where life insurance is not a corporate asset. Now, however, the $6 million of proceeds is treated as a nonoperating asset and is added to value, raising the post-life insurance value to $16 million, and the interests of Harry's estate and Charles to $8 million each (Lines 4-5). After recognizing the repurchase liability of Harry's shares ($8 million), the post-life insurance value of High Point Software is $8 million (Lines 6-7).

The shares are repurchased and new ownership positions are calculated on Lines 9-11. Harry's ownership goes to zero while Charles' holdings rise to 100% of the 50 outstanding shares. This result is the same as above. However, Harry's estate receives $8 million as result of the purchase of his shares, rather than $5 million. Note that the company's value has been reduced from the value prior to Harry's death of $10 million to a post-death value of $8 million. The decrease in value is the result of Harry's value of $8 million, which is in excess of the life insurance proceeds of $6 million, suggesting that the company had to issue a note to Harry's estate or borrow from an outside source to fund the remaining $2 million. So the company is in a more leveraged position as result of the buy-sell transaction than it was before. Charles, on the other hand, owns 100% of the remaining value, or $8 million, rather than $11 million in the prior treatment.

Which Treatment is "Fair"?

It should be clear that the decision on whether or not to treat life insurance as a corporate asset is an important one for all parties. Which treatment is the most "fair?" That depends on what the parties decide. Is it fair for Charles to end up with $11 million in value while Harry's estate only receives $5 million if life insurance is not a corporate asset and serves as a funding vehicle? Charles and the company receive a windfall, but Harry's estate got precisely the amount that Harry would have received had he and Sam decided to sell the company prior to his death.

On the other hand, is it fair to saddle the company with repurchase debt at the moment of its greatest vulnerability: the death of one of its key owners? The answers to these questions may not be immediately clear.

What is clear from this example, however, is that the issue of valuation treatment of life insurance proceeds is far too important not to be addressed in your buy-sell agreement.

The Rest of the Story

Unfortunately, the Harry and Charles story is based on a true story. In the actual situation, Harry's estate (his wife) sued Charles (and the company), demanding that the life insurance owned on Harry's life by the company be considered in the value of the business. After all, "they did everything equally."

Charles claimed they had always agreed that the life insurance would be used by the remaining partner to buy out the other's stock or as a funding vehicle. There was some support for this position in the buy-sell agreement and in related documents, but the support was not clear.

The buy-sell agreement called for two appraisers selected by the company and the estate, respectively, to agree on a third appraiser.

- The third appraiser was called the "neutral appraiser," and his appraisal conclusion was binding on the parties. He was to determine the fair market value of the company as a going concern without allowance for minority interest or marketability discounts. There was no problem with interpretation there.

- The neutral appraiser concluded, based on some "words on the pages" in the agreement, that life insurance should be considered as a corporate asset and added the proceeds to his appraisal conclusion. The "words" were in the preamble to the agreement, which called for a "fair and equitable" value. Charles counter-sued the estate, and the matter proceeded to court.

I was retained by Charles and the company to testify in the case. My testimony related to reviewing the neutral appraiser's report and discussing how buy-sell agreements work, relating some of the language in the agreement to the mechanics of life insurance. The appraiser's conclusion, prior to consideration of life insurance, was reasonable.

The court concluded that the parties got what they asked for – a "fair and equitable" appraisal from a neutral appraiser. Life insurance was included as a corporate asset by the court, which affirmed the neutral appraiser's conclusion.

What did the parties intend in this matter? I don't know. I know what Charles told me and what some documents said. They suggested he could have been right. But the court found otherwise.

What I know is that neither party intended for the death of one of the partners to become the cause of a long, expensive, and friendship-destroying litigation. The entire legal action could have been prevented by a few words in the agreement clearly stating their intent.

Better yet, the entire litigation could have been prevented had Harry and Charles agreed on a single appraiser who valued the company upon selection for purposes of the agreement. The appraiser would have raised the issue of the life insurance, and Harry and Sam would have agreed on what they really wanted to do. That, by the way, is one of the primary reasons I recommend the *Single Appraiser, Select Now and Value Now* appraisal process, which is discussed in detail in Chapter 17.

BUY-SELL AGREEMENT – BET AND DID NOT LOSE

I have chosen our words carefully with this subtitle. You have heard the story about the cobbler's children having no shoes. This next example is illustrative of that expression. Sometimes, there is no better way to illustrate a point than with one's own mistakes.

My own company has had, throughout its history, several ownership structures. It began as a proprietorship, which soon thereafter incorporated with a sole shareholder. Two additional shareholders then came on board. Eventually, one shareholder left, and then there was an extended period of the company having two shareholders. Now, we have the current form of ownership of one shareholder and an employee stock ownership plan.

There were times during this period when the company did not have a buy-sell agreement. At times, there was a fixed-price agreement. The company increased in value at least fourfold during one of the stretches when a fixed-price agreement was in place. Hindsight has brought a great deal of perspective. If anything, the focus on growing the business deflected attention from the buy-sell agreement. If we allowed this situation to perpetuate for so long while knowing better, then we must believe there are other situations that cry out for attention.

In case you're wondering, we have a workable buy-sell agreement now.

My challenge to you is that if you have a fixed-price agreement, move quickly to Chapter 17 and take steps to make your buy-sell agreement workable for the long term.

CHAPTER SIXTEEN

MULTIPLE APPRAISER AGREEMENTS

Pete:	**"After talking about the defining elements of valuation process agreements, how comfortable are you with that single paragraph about hiring appraisers to 'fix' the outdated fixed price?"**
Sam:	"You know the answer to that one."
Pete:	**"So, let's talk about multiple appraiser valuation processes. I think you'll see why I almost always recommend the single appraiser process for buy-sell agreements."**
Sam:	"Let's go. You are on a roll."

Based on my experience, far more buy-sell agreements with valuation processes are multiple appraiser agreements than single appraiser agreements. For reasons that we will see, this is unfortunate.

The interests of shareholders (or former shareholders) and corporations (and remaining shareholders) diverge when buy-sell agreements are triggered.

⊙ This simple fact underscores why it is so important for the parties to reach agreement when their interests are aligned or, at the very least, not misaligned enough to prevent them from agreeing on the future economics of foreseeable trigger events.

- It is virtually impossible to reach agreement on changing a buy-sell agreement after a trigger event has occurred because of the divergent interests of the parties. The logic is simple. If there is not a valid buy-sell agreement, then consider the following example after a triggering event:

  - If you (or your estate) are the seller and I am the buyer, you quite naturally want the highest possible price, and I want the lowest.

  - If you are the buyer and I (or my estate) am the seller, then you naturally want the lowest possible price, and I want the highest.

- Regardless of what we want, if we have a multiple appraiser process buy-sell agreement, neither of us will have any idea what value will be determined by the process, nor how long the process will take, nor how much it will cost.

Nevertheless, the stakes are often so large that the potential differences lead to the retention of attorneys by all sides and litigation follows. Even if there is no formal litigation, the chances are good that the valuation process will be overseen by multiple sets of attorneys looking out for the interests of the various sides to the transaction.

Multiple appraiser agreements call for the selection of two or more appraisers to engage in a process that will develop one, two, or three appraisals whose conclusions form the basis for the final prices. If that process sounds like it might be time consuming, cumbersome, and expensive, you are right. As we will see, such processes can also be divisive and foster litigation.

For purposes of overview, I've categorized multiple appraiser processes into four types, depending on the role of the third appraiser to be selected.

- Third appraiser as a *reconciler*

- Third appraiser as a *determiner*

◎ Third appraiser as a *judge*

◎ Third appraiser as a *mediator*

Before we discuss these potential roles for the third appraiser and outline how each of the processes works, let's understand the underlying thinking that gives rise to these general types of agreements.

Thought Processes Behind Multiple Appraiser Agreements

Multiple appraiser agreements are intended to bring reason and resolution to the valuation process based on prior agreement of the parties. However, intentions and reality do not always match up.

In the real world, motivations – whether actual or perceived – are embedded in many process agreements. These motivations are clear for buyers and sellers whose interests are obviously different. The motivations for the appraisers are less clear. Appraisers are supposed to be independent of the parties. Nevertheless, based on my experience, it is rare for the appraiser retained to represent a seller to reach a valuation conclusion that is lower than that reached by the appraiser for the buyer. This does not necessarily imply that one or both appraisers are biased. Consider the following possibilities:

◎ Valuation reflects both art and science, and is the result of the exercise of judgment. Most multiple appraiser buy-sell agreements call for averaging the first two appraisal conclusions if they are within 10% of each other. Given the potential for differences in judgments, a range of 10% is too small. I'll discuss this in more detail later.

• Appraisers try to estimate the kind of value specified in buy-sell agreements. Consider the real world of actual transactions. In a typical auction process for a company, the range from the low bid to the high bid may be 50% to 100% or more, based on the varying interests and motivations of the buyers in the market at the time.

- The valuation process may foster the appearance or perception of bias by creating the expectation that two appraisers will reach conclusions so close to each other. In other words, if the threshold difference for averaging is 10% and the likelihood of this result is small, even under ideal circumstances, it is not unusual for each side to think that the other side's appraisal conclusion (and appraiser) is biased.

⊚ The buy-sell agreement may be unclear as to the engagement definition. For example, language in some buy-sell agreements is so unclear as to allow or cause one appraiser to reach a conclusion at the strategic control (highest) level of value and the other at the nonmarketable minority (lowest) level (see Figure 8).

- The two independent appraisers who interpret the agreement differently from a valuation perspective may reach conclusions that are widely, or even wildly, disparate.

- If this happens, both sides will likely believe that the other side's appraisal conclusion and appraiser are biased.

Legal counsel for each side desires to protect the interests of their clients. As such, in the context of buy-sell agreements, the thinking may occur as follows:

> "If my client is the seller, we need to be able to select 'our' appraiser because the company will select its appraiser. Since I am concerned that the company will try to influence its appraiser on the downside, I want to be able to try to influence our appraiser on the upside. Since we are selling and they are buying, this is only natural."

For purposes of this discussion, if the two appraisals are not sufficiently close together, then they can be viewed as advocating the positions of the seller and buyer, respectively. All the parties and their legal counsel may begin to think:

> "What is needed now is a 'truly' independent appraiser to finalize the process."

I call this entire process, "One, two, three appraiser, Rock!"

Many process agreements call for the two appraisers to select a third appraiser who is mutually acceptable to them because:

> "Surely, if 'our' appraiser and 'their' appraiser work together, they can select a truly independent appraiser to break the log jam since neither side has been successful in influencing the outcome of the process. But, now that we have a third appraiser, what should his or her role be?"

The role of the third appraiser will be determined from the agreement reached by the parties. Consider the following without putting names to the possibilities:

- The third appraiser's conclusion might be averaged with that of the conclusion closest to his own. The first two appraisers will know this on the front end because it is part of the agreement, so they should be motivated to provide independent conclusions. No one desires to have the outlier (ignored) conclusion.

- The third appraiser's conclusion might be averaged with the other two since the first two conclusions create a potentially broad range (i.e., more than the 10% threshold difference). However, averaging the three conclusions could provide too much influence to an outlier conclusion, whether high or low.

- The third appraiser might be required to select, in his opinion, the more reasonable of the first two conclusions.

Surely, this should tend to influence the first two appraisers to reach more similar conclusions. It would be embarrassing to have provided the conclusion that was not accepted.

⊛ Some processes provide for selection of the first two appraisers whose sole function is to mutually agree on the third appraiser, whose conclusion will be binding. Then, all the pressure falls on the third appraiser.

In every case, the parties either discuss the logic for the process or accept the logic suggested by counsel or implied in the agreement. And while each of these logics may have some merit, in practice none of them really work.

I speak here from personal experience, having been involved in multiple appraiser processes in virtually all of the possible roles (first, second, or third). Clients sometimes do attempt to influence the appraisers, either in blatant or subtle fashion. This is to be expected and is not nefarious. Clients are naturally influenced by their desire for conclusions that are favorable to them. The purpose of process buy-sell agreements, however, regardless of their limitations, should be to reach *reasonable* conclusions.

I have said many times to young appraisers, "Don't be surprised if a client tells you or hints at the appraisal result they desire." In most cases, an appraiser's clients are parties with particular interests in appraisal outcomes. They cannot help that. What is important in these situations is for the appraiser to provide independent conclusions of value – ones that he or she can support and defend.

It is now time to put names to the various multiple appraiser processes.

Third Appraiser as Reconciler

Two appraisers are retained initially to provide appraisals, and a third appraiser is selected, if needed, to resolve disparate valuation conclusions.

1. The buying party typically retains one appraiser and the selling party another appraiser.

2. Both appraisers then provide valuation opinions according to the time schedule specified in the agreement or agreed to by the parties.

3. If the conclusions are within some percentage specified percentage of each other (10% is almost always specified), the buy-sell price is determined by the average of the two conclusions.

4. If the conclusions are more than the selected percentage apart, the two appraisers are generally called upon to select a third appraiser who also provides a valuation conclusion.

5. Often, this third conclusion is averaged with the nearest of the first two, and that average becomes the price.

6. Occasionally, if all three appraisal conclusions are sufficiently close together (you pick the percentage), the price for the agreement is the average of all three conclusions.

7. Sometimes, the lower of the first two appraisals becomes a lower bound with the higher becoming the upper bound, regardless of the third appraiser's conclusion. For example, if the third appraiser's conclusion exceeded the upper bound, the higher of the first two appraisals would become the value.

As we will see in Figure 12, the role of the third appraiser is always to bring the valuation process to conclusion. With the Third Appraiser as Reconciler, the third appraiser is not necessary if the first two reach similar conclusions. The third appraiser is brought in to resolve differences and to cause the process to reach a conclusion by reconciling with one or both of the first two appraisals.

Third Appraiser as Determiner

With the Third Appraiser as Determiner, two appraisers are retained initially.

1. With this variation, the buying party retains one appraiser and the selling party another. These appraisers do not provide valuation opinions. Their sole stated role is to select a mutually agreeable third independent appraiser (the determiner).

2. The third appraiser provides the sole valuation opinion that determines the price. This process foreshadows the single appraiser process that I advocate.

In practice, the first and second appraisers often work on behalf of their clients to help inform the third appraiser. This role is often not spelled out in the buy-sell agreement, but it is typically arranged by the clients with the appraisers.

Third Appraiser as Judge

Two appraisers are selected to provide appraisals, and the third appraiser picks the "better" appraisal.

1. The buying party retains one appraiser and the selling party selects another. Both provide valuation conclusions.

2. If the appraisal conclusions are within a predetermined percentage of each other, the price per the agreement is determined by the average of the two.

3. If the conclusions are sufficiently apart, the two original appraisers must then select a third independent appraiser.

4. The third appraiser acts as "judge" and selects which of the two appraisals they believe to be the most reasonable valuation, and this becomes the price per the buy-sell agreement.

This process may sound like it is efficient and that it should work. However, few agreements using this process specify how the third appraiser will communicate his or her conclusion. It can be particularly unsatisfying (and frustrating) for one side when the other side's conclusion is selected and there is no explanation as to why it was preferred.

Third Appraiser as Mediator

There are several possibilities to the mediation category, all of which are designed to facilitate resolution with the first two appraisers. Two appraisers are selected and they provide valuation conclusions. If their conclusions are within the specified range (10% in most agreements), the price is determined as the average of the two conclusions. If not, the two appraisers are required to work together to reach a mutually acceptable conclusion. Two ways this process could work include:

1. **Negotiation.** If the two appraisers can resolve their differences in direct negotiation and agree on a conclusion, their agreed-upon value becomes the price for the agreement. If they are not successful, then the agreement may call for the selection of a third appraiser, whose role would be that of the reconciler, determiner, or judge as outlined previously. In the negotiation form, there is no mediation role for the third appraiser.

2. **Mediation.** If the two appraisers can resolve their differences and agree on a conclusion, their agreed-upon value becomes the price for the agreement.

   - If they are not successful, the agreement may call for a third appraiser to be selected who will mediate the differences between the first two appraisers.

   - If the mediation is successful in reaching agreement, this conclusion becomes the price for the agreement.

- If the mediation is not successful, the mediator may become the third appraiser.

- The agreement could also call for the first two appraisers, or the first two and the mediator, to agree on another appraiser to become the third appraiser.

- In either event, the third (or fourth) appraiser's role would be that of the reconciler, determiner, or judge as outlined previously.

Process Overview

It has been said that a picture is worth a thousand words. The following figure provides a picture of the Third Appraiser as Reconciler process. The picture illustrates a number of key decision points where time can pass. Multiple appraiser processes are seldom concluded in less than six to nine months. Often, they take one to two years or more.

Figure 12 illustrates the layers of uncertainty in a three appraiser process with the third appraiser as the reconciler. The trigger event occurs at the top of the figure and then time passes until each step of the process occurs. What is certain about a process like this is that no one will know the outcome of the process until the third appraiser's opinion is finalized. This lingering uncertainty over the ultimate outcome is unhealthy and unpleasant for all parties in most multiple appraiser processes.

All of the general forms of multiple appraiser agreements either call for, or potentially call for, the selection of a third appraiser. What is the role of the third appraiser? The role of the third appraiser is to bring resolution to the valuation process, whether as reconciler, determiner, judge, mediator, or otherwise.

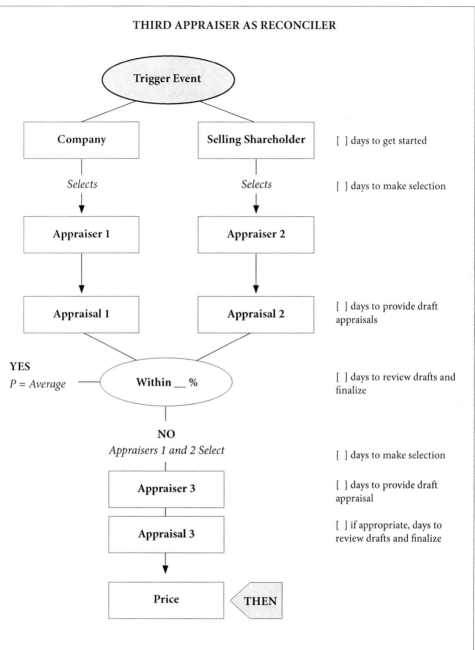

THIRD APPRAISER AS RECONCILER

Trigger Event

Company   Selling Shareholder   [ ] days to get started

Selects   *Selects*   [ ] days to make selection

Appraiser 1   Appraiser 2

Appraisal 1   Appraisal 2   [ ] days to provide draft appraisals

YES
P = Average   Within __ %   [ ] days to review drafts and finalize

NO
Appraisers 1 and 2 Select   [ ] days to make selection

Appraiser 3   [ ] days to provide draft appraisal

Appraisal 3   [ ] if appropriate, days to review drafts and finalize

Price   THEN

- ⊚   Average with the other two conclusions (gives credence to outliers)
- ⊚   Average with the closer of Appraisal 1 and Appraisal 2
- ⊚   The conclusions of Appraisal 1 and 2 may establish upper and lower bounds for final price

FIGURE 12

In many processes, the ox is already in the ditch when the third appraiser is named. For example, there are two appraisals with conclusions more than 10% (as in most agreements) apart. Whether the variations relate to differing understandings or interpretations of the assignment definition, to valuation assumptions and judgments, or to actual bias, the third appraiser is expected to get the ox out of the ditch. The third appraiser's valuation is the tool to reconcile the differences.

What if, however, the differences are irreconcilable? One way of addressing these issues with multiple appraiser agreements is to consider employing single appraiser agreements. Before addressing single appraiser agreements, however, we need to understand the potential advantages and disadvantages of multiple appraiser process buy-sell agreements in order to put my single appraiser recommendation into perspective. With this understanding in mind, we are then in position to evaluate single appraiser alternatives.

Advantages

Multiple appraiser buy-sell agreements have some apparent advantages, although each of the potential advantages can have a downside.

1. They provide a *defined structure* or process for determining the price at which future transactions will occur.

    *   The defined structure of a multiple appraiser agreement may not be well-defined if it contains unclear, ambiguous, or conflicting instructions.

2. All parties to the agreements know, at least *generally*, what the process will entail.

    *   Actually, the parties may *think* they know what will happen with the process. It is one thing to know that your process calls for the use of multiple appraisers and quite another to understand how that process will actually work.

3. Multiple appraiser agreements are fairly common and *generally understood* by attorneys. Many believe that process agreements are better than fixed-price or formula agreements, particularly for substantial companies. And multiple appraiser processes exist in many available templates used by attorneys to draft buy-sell agreements.

    •   Again, while some attorneys may have a general understanding of how a multiple appraiser process might work, not many have significant experience with their actual operation.

4. Parties to such agreements tend to think that they are *protected by the process* since they will get to select "their" appraiser.

    •   This benefit can be illusory. During cross-examination in a recent case involving a buy-sell agreement dispute, for example, I had to clarify the meaning of this point. The thrust of the questions was that since the benefit was illusory, it must be of no real benefit and therefore of no importance at all. To clarify, there should be no substantive benefit to selecting "our appraiser" if the process works like it should. Nevertheless, the ability to make or to participate in that selection is always important to clients.

Disadvantages

There are several disadvantages to multiple appraiser buy-sell agreements:

1. **The price is not determined now.** The actual value, or price, is left to be addressed at a future time, i.e., upon the occurrence of a trigger event. At any time prior to a trigger event and at the end of a potentially lengthy appraisal process, no one knows what the outcome will be.

2. **There is potential for dissatisfaction with the process, the result, or both, for all parties.** Multiple appraiser process agreements are designed with the best of intentions, but as we are beginning to see, they have a number of potential flaws. At best, they are time consuming and expensive. At worst, they are fraught with potential for discord, disruption, and devastating emotional issues for one or all parties.

3. **There is danger of advocacy with multiple appraiser agreements.** Even if there is no advocacy on the part of the appraisers, the presumption or perception of advocacy may taint the process from the viewpoint of one or more participants. One thing is quite clear: The parties in a multiple appraiser process definitely want "their" appraisers to be their advocates.

4. **There is considerable uncertainty regarding the process.** All parties to a multiple appraiser agreement experience uncertainty about how the process will work, even if they have seen another such process in the past. In my experience, the process, as it actually operates, is different in virtually every case, even with seemingly similar agreements. This is true because the parties – including the seller, company management, and its directorate – and the appraisers are all different and react differently in each situation.

5. **There is considerable uncertainty as to the final price.** The price is not determined until the end of the process. As a result, there is great and ongoing uncertainty regarding the price at which such future transactions will occur. First, before a triggering event occurs, no one has any idea what the price would be in the event that one did occur. Second, there can be great uncertainty regarding the ultimate price for many months or even years following a trigger event.

6. **Process problems are not identified until the process is invoked.** Remember that five (and potentially six) defining elements are necessary to determine the price (value) at which shares are purchased pursuant to process buy-sell agreements. Problems with agreements – such as a failure to identify the standard of value or the level of value, or the failure to define the qualifications of appraisers who are eligible to provide opinions, or the appraisal standards they are to follow – are deferred until a trigger event happens. At that time, the interests of the parties are financially adverse, and problems tend to be magnified. *Based on my experience, the failure of multiple appraiser agreements to "pretest" the process can be the most significant disadvantage on this list.*

7. **Multiple appraiser agreements can be expensive.** The cost of appraisals prepared in contentious, potentially litigious situations tends to be considerably higher than for appraisals conducted in the normal course of business.

8. **Multiple appraiser agreements are time-consuming.** The typical appraisal process takes at least 60 to 90 days after appraisers are retained. The search for qualified appraisers can itself take considerable time. If a third appraiser is required, there will be additional time for his or her selection, as well as for the preparation of the third appraisal. It is not unusual for multiple appraiser processes to drag on for six months to a year or more – sometimes much more.

9. **Multiple appraiser agreements are distracting for management.** The appraisal process for a private company is intrusive. Appraisers require that substantial information be developed. They also visit with management, both in person and on the telephone, as part of their appraisal procedures. I recently worked with the CEO of a sizeable

private company to determine the price for the purchase of a 50% interest of his family business. The selling shareholder hired another qualified business appraiser, and we both provided appraisals. The parties agreed that the appraisers would attempt to negotiate a settlement rather than invoking the burdensome formal procedures of the buy-sell agreement. Our appraisals were about 10% apart, and the parties agreed to average them. During the nearly three months that this "less burdensome" process was underway, the CEO (and his CFO and his COO) could scarcely think about anything else.

10. **Multiple appraiser agreements are potentially devastating for selling shareholders.** If the seller is the estate of a former shareholder, there is not only uncertainty regarding the value of the stock, but family members are involved in a valuation dispute with the friends and associates of their deceased loved one. Combine these issues with the fact that some agreements require that selling shareholders pay for their share (side) of the appraisal process, and there is even more cause for distress.

We summarize the disadvantages of multiple appraiser process agreements in Figure 13 for comparison with other options as the discussion progresses.

Concluding Observations

Based on my experience, multiple appraiser process agreements seem to be the norm for substantial private companies and in joint venture agreements among corporate venture partners. The standard forms or templates found for process agreements at many law firms include variations of multiple appraiser processes similar to those described previously.

Business appraisers participate in multiple appraiser buy-sell agreement processes with some frequency. Speaking personally, I have been the

	DISADVANTAGES	MULTIPLE APPRAISERS
1.	Price not determined now	x
2.	Potential for dissatisfaction with the process for all parties	x
3.	Danger of advocacy	x
4.	Uncertainty over what will happen when a trigger event occurs	x
5.	Uncertainty over final price if the process is invoked	x
6.	Problems or issues with definition of value, qualifications of appraisers, or any other aspects of the operation of the agreements are deferred until a trigger event – when the interests of the parties are adverse	x
7.	Expensive	x
8.	Time-consuming	x
9.	Distracting for management	x
10.	Potentially devastating for affected shareholders and their families	x

FIGURE 13

appraiser working on behalf of selling shareholders and companies, and I have been the third appraiser selected by the other two on other occasions. As the third appraiser, I have been required to provide opinions where the process called for the averaging of my conclusion with the other two as well as averaging with the conclusion nearest mine. I have also been asked to pick the better appraisal, in my opinion, given the definition of value in agreements. And I have been the third appraiser who provided the only appraisal.

These experiences are mentioned to emphasize that the disadvantages of multiple appraiser appraisal processes outlined here are quite real. I have seen at close hand every disadvantage in the list above.

There is a better way for most companies to determine value for purposes of their buy-sell agreements using a single appraiser.

EVERYONE HAS TO VALUE THE SAME COMPANY

A number of years ago, I received a call from two gentlemen. The first was a business appraiser from Texas and the second was an investment banker from a now defunct investment bank that was major at the time. They had each been retained by substantial private companies: a multi-billion-dollar U.S. company and a similar-sized European company that were 50-50 joint venture partners in a $100 million distribution business.

One partner was buying out the other pursuant to a buy-sell agreement that called for three appraisers to render valuations; the closest two were to be averaged for the result. The investment banker worked on behalf of the buying party, and the Texas appraiser worked on behalf of the selling party. I was selected as the "neutral" appraiser.

All appraisers conducted simultaneous management visits. Management representatives from the parent companies of the joint venture partners were present, as well as counsel for each. Management of the joint venture was present. We (the appraisers) asked questions of joint venture management, and anyone who desired could respond. As the third appraiser, I got to ask the final questions on each topic of investigation.

The buy-sell agreement called for the appraisers to render opinions of the fair market value of the enterprise on a going concern basis as of a date that was clearly specified. It was clear that the appraisers should not apply discounts for lack of control or for lack of marketability. All appraisers received the same financial information and relied on the same financial statements.

During the management interview, the buying party's management indicated that they might cease supplying a significant portion of product to the resulting entity following the transaction and that this would have an adverse impact on value. This possibility was discussed with all parties present in the same room. I read from the buy-sell agreement the instructions requiring the appraisers to value the company as of a specific date. At that date, there were no plans for any termination of supply arrangements by the buying party.

The Texas appraiser and I valued the company as it existed on the valuation date with its outlook unaffected by any change in supply arrangements. The investment banker did a discounted cash flow analysis assuming that a significant portion of existing supply lines would be terminated. On a value scale of 1 to 10, the Texas appraiser and I were 9 and 10 (or 10 and 9). The investment banker's conclusion was at 4. The binding conclusion was therefore 9.5.

I received a call from the investment banker. He was angry with me for not using the self-serving projections of his client. He told me that if he had known what I'd do, he never would have agreed for me to be the third appraiser. I told him that if he had valued the same company, he would have been in the same range.

> My challenge to you is to take whatever steps are necessary to avoid such issues with your buy-sell agreement. The investment banker was not independent, had no experience in private company appraisal, and no valuation training or credentials. The last thing that any valuation process needs is one or more appraisers who are advocates for their clients rather than advocates of their own independent valuation conclusions.

Chapter Seventeen

The Recommended Structure: Single Appraiser, Select Now and Value Now

Pete:	**"Sam, I think it is time to talk about the kind of buy-sell agreement that I think is most appropriate for you."**
Sam:	"After learning what's wrong with our agreement, I agree!"
Pete:	**"Right now, you have a fixed-price agreement with a dated price. Your agreement also has a multiple appraiser process that will likely not work. The solution is to get together with your fellow owners and to agree on a new buy-sell agreement. What I recommend is a *Single Appraiser, Select Now and Value Now* process."**
Sam:	"What do you mean by that?"
Pete:	**"Let me outline the process for you:**
	1. **Select a qualified independent business appraiser. You, George, William, and Don get together and work at this a bit. Obtain qualifications information. Ask for references. Talk to the most qualified persons. You should be able to agree on an appraiser.**

2. Have the appraiser provide a draft valuation. The appraiser will ask you what standard of value and level of value the company wants for the agreement. My recommendation is that you tell him or her that fair market value is the standard of value, and that financial control be considered as the appropriate level of value.

3. Review the draft. Once you have the draft appraisal, all of you should read the draft and go over any questions you have with the appraiser. If you don't understand something, as I often say, 'Don't stand for it.' Just get comfortable with the methodology and the conclusion. You should all be sure that the level of value and financial control is what you want in your agreement.

4. Talk about other terms. We've talked about a number of things you might want to consider when you review your agreement. You can use the *Buy-Sell Agreement Audit Checklist* as a guide.

5. Involve your attorney, who will need to help in revising your buy-sell agreement.

6. Have the attorney redraft your buy-sell agreement. The new agreement will name the appraiser and the basic qualifications you agreed upon in the selection process. When the appraiser finalizes the appraisal, the conclusion will become the initial price for your new agreement.

7. Obtain annual or periodic reappraisals. The agreement should call for an annual reappraisal, which should be part of the appraiser's engagement letter with the company. The annual reappraisals will become the new, updated prices for your agreement when they are finalized each year (or every other year at the least)."

Sam: "Wow! That's a lot to absorb so quickly."

Pete: "It really isn't so bad if you break it down into pieces and work on it. But it really is worth the effort."

Sam: "I'm beginning to believe you."

Single Appraiser, Select Now and Value Now

The *Single Appraiser, Select Now and Value Now* buy-sell agreement valuation process is the one I recommend for most successful closely held and family businesses. For the reasons we have discussed at length, I prefer this single appraiser process as the best available alternative for fixed-price, formula, and multiple appraiser agreements.

This chapter mentions two other single appraiser processes:

⊚ *Single Appraiser, Select and Value at Trigger Event*

⊚ *Single Appraiser, Select Now and Value at Trigger Event*

Our focus is on the *Single Appraiser, Select Now and Value Now* process. The other two processes are mentioned because I have seen them in agreements. As we will see, in either of these alternatives, either the initial valuation or both the initial valuation and selection of appraiser are postponed into the indefinite future – i.e., until a trigger event occurs. This postponement of the appraiser selection and initial valuation create substantial uncertainties and potential for disagreement or dispute. In my opinion, these two other single appraiser processes are not ideal substitutes for fixed-price, formula or multiple appraiser process agreements.

In the *Single Appraiser, Select Now and Value Now*, the appraiser is not only named in the agreement, but he or she is engaged to provide an initial appraisal for purposes of the agreement.

- **Select now.** I have long recommended that parties creating buy-sell agreements name the appraiser at the time of agreement. This way, all parties have a voice and can sign off on the selection of the appraiser no matter how difficult the process of reaching agreement.

- **Value now.** Once selected, the chosen appraiser provides a baseline appraisal for purposes of the agreement. I suggest that the appraisal be rendered in draft form to all parties to the agreement, and that everyone has a reasonable period of time to provide comments for consideration before the report is finalized.

- **Value each year (or two) thereafter.** Ideally, the selected appraiser will provide annual revaluations for buy-sell agreement purposes.

The *Single Appraiser, Select Now and Value Now* process provides several distinct advantages relative to other process agreements, including:

- The structure and process, in addition to being defined in the agreement, will be known to all parties to the agreement in advance.

- The selected appraiser will be viewed as independent with respect to the process; otherwise, he or she would not have been named. At the very least, the suspicion of bias is minimized.

- The appraiser's valuation approaches and methodologies are seen first hand by the parties before any triggering event occurs.

- The appraiser's valuation conclusion is known at the outset of the agreement by all parties and becomes the agreement's price until the next appraisal, or until a trigger event between recurring appraisals occurs.

- The process is observed at the outset; therefore, all parties know what will happen when a trigger event happens.

- The appraiser must interpret the valuation terms of the agreement in conducting the initial appraisal. Any lack of clarity in the valuation-defining terms ("the words on the pages") will be revealed and can be corrected to the parties' mutual satisfaction.

- Having provided an initial valuation opinion, the appraiser must maintain independence with respect to the process and render future valuations consistent with the instructions in the agreement.

- Because the appraisal process is exercised at least once, or on a recurring basis, it should go smoothly when employed at trigger events and be less time-consuming and less expensive than other alternatives.

One further element can improve the *Single Appraiser, Select Now and Value Now* option even more – regular reappraisals. In my opinion, most companies with substantial value (beginning at $2 to $3 million of value) should have an annual revaluation for their agreements. For most such companies, the cost of the appraisal process is insignificant relative to the certainty provided by maintaining the pricing provisions on a current basis. Owners who view the cost of an annual reappraisal as excessive should have the reappraisals every other year. An overview of the *Single Appraiser, Select Now and Value Now* process is provided in Figure 14.

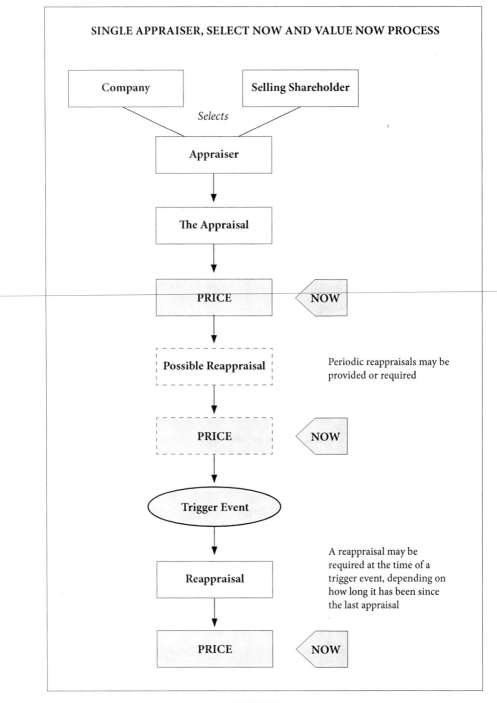

FIGURE 14

Additional benefits from annual or periodic reappraisal for buy-sell agreements include:

- **The parties will tend to gain confidence in the process.** The selected appraisal firm should provide valuations that are generally consistent with prior opinions, taking into account relevant changes in the company, the industry, the economy, and other relevant factors. Subsequent appraisals should be reconciled with prior appraisals so that all parties understand why value has changed.

- **The parties will know the most current value for the buy-sell agreement.** This can be beneficial for a company's planning purposes, for example, facilitating the maintenance of adequate life insurance on the lives of appropriate shareholders. The periodic appraisal will also be helpful for the planning purposes of shareholders.

- **The *Single Appraiser, Select Now and Value Now* process with annual reappraisals facilitates the estate planning objectives of the shareholders at relatively low incremental cost.** If the buy-sell agreement calls for an enterprise level of value (marketable minority or financial control), the appraiser can provide a supplemental appraisal at the nonmarketable minority level for gift and estate tax purposes. This supplemental appraisal would, of course, have to consider the impact of the buy-sell agreement on the value of nonmarketable minority interests. Consult with your tax attorney to be sure that the buy-sell agreement price is determinative of value for estate tax purposes.

- **Enhanced confidence for all parties.** Importantly, because the appraisals are recurring in nature, the appraisal firm's knowledge of a company's business and industry will grow over time, which should further enhance the confidence all parties have in the process and conclusion of value.

In all cases, if the most current appraisal is more than a specified amount of time old, then the agreements should provide for a reappraisal upon the occurrence of a trigger event.

Figure 15 shows the 10 critical disadvantages of multiple appraiser valuation processes relative to their consideration with single appraiser processes. Focus on the disadvantages in the multiple appraisers column and the *Single Appraiser, Select Now and Value Now* column. The middle two columns will come into perspective in the brief discussion of the other two single appraiser processes below.

	DISADVANTAGES	MULTIPLE APPRAISER	SINGLE APPRAISER		
			Select and Value at Trigger Event	Select Now and Value at Trigger Event	Select Now and Value Now
1.	Price not determined now	x	x	x	
2.	Potential for dissatisfaction with the process for all parties	x	x	x	Minimized
3.	Danger of advocacy	x	x	Minimized	Minimized
4.	Uncertainty over what will happen when a trigger event occurs	x	x	x	Minimized
5.	Uncertainty over final price if the process is invoked	x	x	x	Minimized
6.	Problems or issues with definition of value, qualifications of appraisers, or any other aspects of the operation of the agreements are deferred until a trigger event – when the interests of the parties are adverse	x	x	x	Minimized
7.	Expensive	x			
8.	Time-consuming	x			
9.	Distracting for management	x			
10.	Potentially devastating for affected shareholders and their families	x			

FIGURE 15

1. **Price is not determined now.** The *Single Appraiser, Select Now and Value Now* is the only valuation process that provides information about the buy-sell agreement price now. Current information enables the parties to plan and eliminates the great uncertainty about value that builds with the passage of time.

2. **Potential for dissatisfaction with the process for all parties.** There will always be potential for dissatisfaction. Buyers naturally want lower prices and sellers want higher prices. However, if the process works as it should, all parties are much more likely to believe that the prices created by the buy-sell process are reasonable. The *Single Appraiser, Select Now and Value Now* process minimizes this uncertainty.

3. **Danger (or perception) of advocacy.** At the outset, it is possible that one or more parties might believe that the selected single appraiser in a *Single Appraiser, Select Now and Value Now* process could be biased. Such perceptions would likely be minimized or mitigated over time as the appraiser provides subsequent appraisals that can be reconciled with changes in the company, the industry, the economy, and other broad factors. Also, all parties should become more comfortable with the process.

4. **Uncertainty over what will happen when a trigger event occurs.** With a single appraiser who is selected in advance and who provides recurring reappraisals, there should be little, if any, uncertainty about the process that will be invoked when trigger events occur. The process is seen on a recurring basis by all parties. This advantage is minimized or even eliminated by the *Single Appraiser, Select Now and Value Now* process.

5. **Uncertainty over the final price if the process is invoked.** Given that there is a baseline appraisal and the potential for

reappraisals over time with the *Single Appraiser, Select Now and Value Now* process, much of the uncertainty regarding the price at a triggering event should be eliminated. The price should be reasonably consistent with changes in the company's earnings, industry multiples, and other factors familiar to the parties, assuming that the selected appraiser continues to provide appraisals on a consistent basis.

6. **Problems or issues with definition of value, qualifications of appraisers, or any other aspects of the operation of the agreements are deferred until a trigger event – when the interests of the parties are adverse.** Clearly, any issues with the valuation process would be identified and fixed at the outset or along the way. The process should be clear and well-understood, so issues of this nature should be minimized or eliminated using a *Single Appraiser, Select Now and Value Now* valuation process.

7. **Expensive.** Multiple appraiser processes, with two or three appraisers, multiple sets of lawyers, and occasionally other professionals, as well, can be quite expensive. When, as often happens, these processes become contentious, they become enormously expensive. The *Single Appraiser, Select Now and Value Now* process virtually eliminates the potential for cost expansion. Recurring reappraisals are normally less expensive than the initial appraisal, and since all parties know what will happen at a trigger event, there is little need for excessive legal or appraisal intervention with the process.

8. **Time-consuming.** A reappraisal would be conducted in the normal course of business following a trigger event in the *Single Appraiser, Select Now and Value Now* process. It stands to reason that this process would be of shorter duration than a multiple appraiser process being initiated for the first time under adverse circumstances.

9. **Distracting for management.** As with the prior disadvantage, it should be apparent that a reappraisal conducted in the normal course of business would be less distracting to management than a (likely) contentious valuation process being initiated for the first time.

10. **Potentially devastating for affected shareholders and their families.** With the *Single Appraiser, Select Now and Value Now* process, all shareholders know, in advance, what the valuation process will be like. They also know, at least generally, the range in which the valuation conclusion will occur because of knowledge of prior appraisals and current company performance.

In summary, the *Single Appraiser, Select Now and Value Now* process eliminates the first disadvantage of multiple appraiser processes, because value is known now. It minimizes (or eliminates) uncertainties associated with the next five disadvantages above. Finally, it should eliminate issues related with the last four disadvantages.

This form of single appraiser process is, based on my experience over some 30 years, the most reasonable valuation process for most closely held and family businesses.

Single Appraiser, Select and Value at Trigger Event

In *Single Appraiser, Select and Value at Trigger Event* agreements, the selection of the single appraiser is called for at the time of a triggering event. The selected appraiser provides the valuation based on his interpretation of the language in the buy-sell agreement. The single appraiser's valuation conclusion then sets the price for purposes of the buy-sell agreement.

The advantages of a single appraiser process are similar to those of the multiple appraiser processes previously outlined.

- ⊚ It provides a defined structure or process for determining the price at which future transactions will occur.

- ⊚ All parties to the agreement know in advance, at least generally, what the process will be.

- ⊚ The cost of the process, if not known precisely in advance, is reasonably definable.

- ⊚ The general process is fairly commonly known and understood by attorneys. The single appraiser process is simpler than multiple appraiser processes since only one appraiser must be selected.

- ⊚ Parties to single appraiser agreements should believe they are protected by the process since they will have a voice in the selection of the appraiser. All sides have a role to ensure that an independent appraiser is selected, i.e., one who will provide a balanced analysis and a "fair" valuation rendered in accordance with the agreed upon defining elements and taking into account the interests of both sides during the appraisal process.

The company (its CEO or CFO) may be the primary driver in the process of selecting the appraiser. It is therefore important that each party subject to the agreement has an active role in the selection process (probably veto power). This is why it is essential to specify the qualifications of the appraiser in advance. The pool of potential appraisers should include only those that obviously meet the stated qualifications. Both sides must have input and agree, or there can definitely be a perception of bias, at least initially.

There are, however, disadvantages specific to the *Single Appraiser, Select and Value at Trigger Event* process as shown in Figure 15.

There is an additional disadvantage of the *Select and Value at Trigger Event* variation. Once a trigger event occurs, the interests of the parties diverge. It is possible that they will be unable to agree on the selection of an appraiser.

Therefore, it is necessary to have an alternate appraiser selection process, perhaps through mediation or arbitration, to select the appraiser. Processes that begin in this fashion have a higher probability of problems than when the parties reach agreement before a triggering event.

Nevertheless, on balance, the *Select and Value at Trigger Event* process eliminates a number of the disadvantages of multiple appraiser agreements. These processes are less time consuming and less expensive. They should therefore be less distracting for management. And they have the potential to be less worrisome for families of deceased (or otherwise departed) owners.

Single Appraiser, Select Now and Value at Trigger Event

The third single appraiser process is *Select Now and Value at Trigger Event*. The appraiser is named in the agreement and will be called upon to provide the required appraisals at the time of future trigger events. At the time the agreement is created (or an older agreement is revised), the parties may discuss potential appraisers (appraisal firms), interview one or more firms, and select a mutually agreeable appraiser/firm. This firm is written into the agreement as the named appraiser.

The *Select Now and Value at Trigger Event* form of agreement eliminates the future uncertainty of selecting an appraiser, which is an improvement over *Select and Value at Trigger Event* agreements, but the other uncertainties and disadvantages remain. However, concerns over the degree of perceived appraiser advocacy should be minimized since the parties have time to agree on the selected appraiser absent the pressure of a trigger event.

SINGLE APPRAISER, SELECT NOW AND VALUE NOW (AND ANNUALLY THEREAFTER)

I've been advancing the idea of the *Single Appraiser, Select Now and Value Now* process because I know it works. Consider the following:

- There are some 10,000 private companies in the U.S. that have Employee Stock Ownership Plans (ESOPs). Every one of these companies has an appraisal at least annually. In my experience, the buy-sell agreements of most ESOP companies are tied to the annual appraisals and most transactions that occur in the stock of these companies are at their most recent appraised prices.

- Some 20 of my long-standing client companies have had annual appraisals for many years. Their buy-sell agreements and the estate planning of their owners are tied to these annual reappraisals. Many of these companies do not have ESOPs, so they obtain their appraisals voluntarily on the basis of their direct and indirect benefits for the companies and their owners.

- Closer to home, my company, Mercer Capital, is an ESOP company, and we obtain an independent appraisal each year. Our buy-sell agreement is tied to this annual appraisal.

- One client company of 20 years has purchased more than $100 million of stock from employees over the last six years and has sold more than $30 million of stock to employees on the basis of annual appraisals.

I advocate the *Single Appraiser, Select Now and Value Now* process for most buy-sell agreements because it is the only one that will ensure that your buy-sell agreement will work when it is triggered.

CHAPTER EIGHTEEN

OTHER IMPORTANT ASPECTS OF PROCESS BUY-SELL AGREEMENTS

Pete:	**"There are a few other things we need to talk about before I give you a homework assignment."**
Sam:	"I'm sure I'll learn something new."
Pete:	**"I hope so. We just need to talk about a few details for you to think about."**
Sam:	"I can hardly wait."

Several other issues related to valuation should be addressed in your buy-sell agreements. The following discussion is by no means exhaustive, but includes significant items that are helpful in minimizing problems or uncertainties with the operation of valuation process buy-sell agreements. While some of these items may seem obvious when identified, they are quite often overlooked or are unclear in buy-sell agreements.

Financial Statements

It can be helpful to specify the financial statements to be used by the appraiser(s). This is normally done in relation to the "as of" date for the valuation per the agreement. In the absence of specification, the parties must agree on the financial statements to be used, or else the appraiser(s) must decide. Significant differences in valuation conclusions can result from the selection of financial statements of different dates and quality. This confusion should be avoided.

The general rule for any valuation is that appraisers should use information that was known as of the valuation date. That standard has been expanded to include information that was also reasonably knowable.

In this light, possible alternatives for specifying financial statements include:

1. **Most recent audit or the audited financial statements for the most recent fiscal year relative to the valuation date.** Note that there is room for confusion here. Assume that the fiscal year is the calendar year. Suppose that the trigger date for a valuation process is January 15, 2007. The most recent audit was issued as of December 31, 2005 on April 27, 2006. If the buy-sell agreement calls for the use of the most recent audit available on the trigger date, the financial data may be more than one year old as in this example.

   The agreement might specify that if a trigger event occurs between the end of a fiscal year and the issuance of the audit for that year, the appraisers would rely on the audit when it becomes available. That audit would then be used for the rest of the fiscal year.

   In the alternative, if the trigger date was December 15, 2006, the most recent audit would be the 2005 audit issued in April 2006, but internal financial statements for the full year 2006 would be available within weeks, and the audit for 2006 would be available in three or four months, perhaps within the timeframe that appraisals would be prepared.

   Suffice it to say, disagreements over which audit (i.e., which fiscal year) to use as the base for financial analysis could cause material differences in the concluded results.

Note that the confusion could result whether the buy-sell agreement required the use of either the most recent audit or the most recent fiscal year statements.

2. **Trailing 12 months at the most recent quarter-end (month-end) to the "as of" date.** In the absence of specific guidance, many, if not most appraisers, would utilize financial statements for the most recent 12 months as of the quarter-end (or month-end) immediately prior to the trigger date. Use of the trailing 12 months would automatically include consideration of the most recent fiscal year (and audit, if available), and it would also include any routine year-end adjustments for that year-end.

   We generally recommend the use of the trailing 12-month financial statements for the most recent quarter-end preceding the valuation date (or month-end, depending on the completeness and quality of the monthly financial statements).

In the *Single Appraiser, Select Now and Value Now* process, assuming that the appraiser made a reasonable decision regarding financial statements, there would be no disagreement and no discrepancies in conclusions because of such disagreements.

Process Timetables

Many buy-sell agreements provide for unrealistic timetables while others specify no timetables at all. They, therefore, begin with process problems from the outset. The typical buy-sell process contains a number of phases where time is required:

- **Time to get the process started.** It takes time to initiate a valuation process. If the trigger event is the death of a shareholder, no one will be focused on the buy-sell agreement until the passage of a reasonable amount of time. On the other hand, if the triggering event is a planned retirement or termination, the parties may be ready to initiate the buy-sell agreement process immediately.

⊙ **Time to select appraiser(s).** Most process agreements call for the parties to retain an appraiser. If a company or a shareholder is beginning from scratch to select an appraiser(s), it can easily take 30 to 60 days or more to identify firms, review qualifications, interview appraisers, and select an appraiser(s).

- Some agreements allow only 30 days for this process, which may be unrealistic for one party or the other.

- Some agreements are silent regarding the selection process, thereby providing no guidance for the appraisal process to get started (or concluded).

- Many process agreements call for two appraisals at the outset. If they provide valuations within a designated percentage of each other, no further appraisals are required. If not, however, the two initial appraisers must agree on a third appraiser. This process takes time – often considerable time. Some agreements provide timetables for this process and others do not.

- In some agreements, the sole role of the first two appraisers is to select the third appraiser. The same time issues relate to this selection. Allow at least 30 to 60 days for this process.

- The obvious way to avoid this time lag in getting appraisals started is to select the appraiser at the initiation of the buy-sell agreement using the *Single Appraiser, Select Now and Value Now* alternative previously discussed.

⊙ **Time to prepare appraisal(s).** Once selected, the appraiser(s) must prepare their appraisal(s). Appraisal processes normally takes at least 60 to 90 days. I like a clause in engagement letters stating the appraiser will use his or her best efforts to provide a draft valuation report for review within 30 days of an on site visit with management.

- Note that the entire process would still take 60 days or more, depending on how quickly the client responds to the information request and schedules the visit, as well as how long the client takes to review the draft. It takes many companies 30 to 60 days to provide the basic information required to conduct an appraisal prior to the on site visit because the activities of running their businesses get in the way.

- If a third appraiser is retained, this appraiser will require time for his or her process. If this is the only appraisal being provided, the process normally takes from 60 to 90 days. If there have been two appraisals already, the third appraiser may be helped by the fact that the company has already developed most of the information that will be required.

- On the other hand, being the third appraiser can be a fairly dicey situation. In addition to preparing one's own appraisal as the third appraiser, it is also necessary to review the appraisals of the other two firms. Allow at least 60 to as many as 90 days or more for this process.

- While time requirements in buy-sell agreements are seldom binding on appraisers, they are appropriate to reflect the necessary sense of urgency to keep valuation processes moving to completion.

⊚ **Time to review draft appraisals.** The procedures of many appraisal firms call for the preparation of draft reports to be reviewed by management, and in the case of some buy-sell agreements, by all sides. This review process will generally take from 15 to 30 days or more, particularly in contentious situations. In my opinion, the appraiser issuing appraisals in valuation processes for buy-sell agreements should issue draft opinions. The process should allow 15 to 30 days for all sides to review and comment on the draft. All appraisers then have the opportunity to consider all comments prior to finalizing their opinions. Many mistakes can be corrected and misunderstandings avoided by following this procedure. When I am involved in appraisal processes where the review period is not stated in the agreement, I ask the parties to agree to this additional step.

⊚ **Time to arrange financing or to close.** Once the appraisal process has been concluded, it normally takes some time to bring the process to closure. The company may be allowed 30 days, or some reasonable amount of time to close the transaction.

We can summarize the process timelines to get a picture of how the various types of process agreements might look in operation. You may be surprised at how the various processes actually lay out, regardless of what the written timetables suggest. The timelines in Figure 16 are estimated based on actual experiences with the operation of buy-sell agreements. We show approximate timelines for multiple appraiser and single appraiser agreements.

The existence of defined timetables in agreements serves to keep the parties focused on the timeline; however, they are seldom binding.

BUY-SELL AGREEMENT TIMELINES

PROCESS ACTIVITIES (IN DAYS)	MULTIPLE APPRAISER		SINGLE APPRAISER, SELECT NOW AND VALUE NOW	
	Low	High	Low	High
Trigger Event Occurs	0	0	0	0
Time To React	1	30	1	30
Pick Appraiser(s)	30	60	0	0
Provide Appraisal(s)	60	90	30	60
Review Appraisal(s)	15	30	15	30
Earliest Time to Resolution	**106**	**210**	**46**	**120**
Select Other Appraiser(s)	30	60		
Reviews by Appraisers				
Prepare Additional Appraisal(s)	30	60		
Review Appraisals/Reviews	15	30		
Agree on Conclusions	15	30		
Finalize Transaction	0	30		
Additional Time for Process	**90**	**210**	**0**	**0**
Potential Time to Resolution	**196**	**420**	**46**	**120**

FIGURE 16

Figure 16 illustrates timelines for (generalized) multiple appraiser processes, and the *Single Appraiser, Select Now and Value Now* process.

⊙ **Multiple appraiser** processes can be accomplished in the broad range of 100 to 200 days or so *if the initial process involving two appraisers is conclusive.* If it is necessary to select and retain a third appraiser, it is likely that considerable additional time will pass before resolution occurs. It is not surprising for a multiple appraiser process involving three appraisers to take six months to a year or more to complete.

- The *Single Appraiser, Select Now and Value Now* option is potentially the most rapid process option for buy-sell agreements. If a triggering event occurs after the initial appraisal, then the valuation process will be known by all parties, and the appraiser will be familiar with the company. This option should be able to be accomplished within six weeks or so, on the short end, and four months on the longer end.

Note that the estimates here assume that there is no litigation and that the parties are generally cooperating to move the process along.

I am sometimes asked to become involved in valuation processes where the timetables are not specified or those specified are unreasonable. I ask the parties to agree on a new, reasonable timetable so everyone can have reasonable expectations. The bottom line is that it is good to agree on realistic timelines in your buy-sell agreements. It is then easier to ask the various appraisers and other parties to stick to them.

The operation of process buy-sell agreements can take a long time. This means that the process may be a considerable distraction to management, particularly when significant transactions are involved. It should be obvious, but the prolonged operation of a buy-sell agreement can not only be distracting, but also frustrating and confusing to the family of a deceased shareholder or to a terminated employee.

Who Bears the Costs of the Appraisal Process?

Appraisal processes that involve between one and three appraisers can become expensive. This is particularly true when large companies and/or large dollar-value interests are involved. It is even more the case if there is threatened or actual litigation.

So who pays the costs of the appraisal(s)? Some agreements state that the company will pay for its appraiser, and the shareholder will pay for his or her appraiser. I seldom inject opinion into the operation of agreements; however, the company is often in a position of economic advantage relative to a shareholder (or a deceased shareholder's family). Therefore, I suggest consideration of a clause providing that the company pay the appraisal costs of selling shareholder(s). Consider that:

⊚   The company pays for its expenses in pre-tax dollars.

⊚   The company typically experiences an economic benefit from the operation of the agreement. More particularly, the other shareholders experience a net benefit (pro rata increases in their percentages of ownership) from the share repurchase program. There is no corresponding benefit for the selling shareholder (other than liquidity).

⊚   Public and private companies often engage in share repurchase programs. When conducted at reasonable pricing levels (the goal of buy-sell agreements), share repurchase programs provide liquidity to shareholders. They also reduce the number of shares outstanding, increase earnings per share for remaining shareholders, and increase their relative ownership of the enterprise. Value per share for the remaining shareholders then tends to rise. Other than liquidity, which may be desired by selling shareholders, there are no corresponding benefits.

⊚   It is likely that the company is better able to afford a more experienced appraiser than an individual shareholder, creating a potential disadvantage at the outset.

⊚   The shareholder is being asked to pay to realize the value of his or her shares according to the agreement. The agreement calls for a certain price to be received for the shares. The shareholder receives that price, determined by the process, less the expenses of the operation of the process. Therefore, if the shareholder pays appraisal costs, the operation of the agreement does not actually provide the specified price.

It could be argued that this position is too generous to the selling shareholder. After all, if and when the remaining shareholders sell the company, they will incur transaction costs. These costs are the "friction" or transaction costs of changing ownership, including legal and accounting fees, investment banking or brokerage fees, and even appraisal fees. In recognition of the reality of friction costs, the parties could agree that the concluded price for buy-sell agreement purposes will be the appraised price less a transactions cost allowance of a set percentage. The transaction cost allowance would likely be in the range of 2% to 5% or so of the determined value, depending on the size of the business.

If the company agrees to pay appraisal costs of selling shareholder(s) (with or without consideration of a transaction cost allowance), shareholders might be concerned that the selected appraiser would have an allegiance to the company since the company is the financially responsible party. Never mind that all selected appraisers are supposed to be independent. This concern can be addressed by having the appraisal firm's engagement letter with the selling shareholder(s) rather than the company. The company could then be a party to the engagement letter to accept financial responsibility only for fees and, perhaps, indemnification. From the company's viewpoint, it may be appropriate to specify a maximum amount for its responsibility for the shareholder's appraisal expenses.

This issue is moot, of course, if the buy-sell agreement calls for the *Single Appraiser, Select Now and Value Now* option. The company will pay for the initial appraisal and subsequent appraisals.

Who Benefits (or Loses) from Unavoidable (or Avoidable) Delays?

The purpose of buy-sell agreements is to facilitate the sale (and corresponding purchase) of shares following defined trigger events. They do not necessarily contemplate the economic interests of the various parties during the process of their operation.

Buy-sell agreements specify certain trigger events. These events may determine the "as of" date for the required appraisals. Suppose, for example, the death of a shareholder triggers the operation of a buy-sell agreement. The date of death is often the valuation date, or the "as of" date. Or, the valuation date might be set as of the month-end immediately preceding (or following) the date of death.

Now suppose that the operation of the agreement, including time spent dealing with litigation regarding its operation, takes two years to complete. Several questions illustrate potential issues that may need to be addressed in an agreement:

- ⊚ Should the company pay interest from the valuation date to the date of finalization of the transaction? A shareholder who does not receive payment on or near the valuation date clearly incurs an opportunity cost. No funds are available to earn interest or apply to other reinvestment. Arguably, the shareholder still bears the risks of an equity holder during this period with no provision for interim returns and the company has an interest-free loan.

- ⊚ What happens if the company's performance was stellar during the period between the trigger event and the final settlement? Should the valuation date be moved forward?

- ⊚ What happens if the company's performance declined over the same period?

- Who owns the shares following a trigger event? Is the interest of a shareholder converted into a right to receive the buy-sell price as soon as that price is determined for the "as of" date? Or does the shareholder retain ownership of shares until purchased? This may be a legal question. But it is one that can be agreed upon by the parties.

- Do the shares retain their voting rights and can the shareholder vote them if there is a shareholder's meeting prior to the shares being purchased?

- Is the shareholder entitled to receive distributions or dividends until the shares are repurchased? Is the company obligated to maintain its distribution policy (if applicable) during the interim period between the "as of" date and finalization of the process?

- If the company is an S corporation or other tax pass-through entity, does the agreement ensure that the shareholder will receive sufficient distributions to pay shareholder level taxes on corporate earnings for the entire period of ownership?

These questions are best addressed before an agreement's processes are initiated. When agreements are silent, one or both parties can lose.

Appraiser or Appraisal Firm?

Buy-sell agreements with valuation processes call for the selection of business appraisers. The appraisers, not appraisal firms, render valuation opinions. Nevertheless, engagement letters are virtually always executed naming appraisal firms. The question is less significant if appraisers are being retained after a trigger event. They are being retained in real time and provide their opinions in due course.

When employing the *Single Appraiser, Select Now and Value Now* process recommended in this book, it is likely best to retain an appraisal firm. While an individual business appraiser (or more than one, if appropriate) will sign each appraisal, the retention of a firm provides the vehicle for smooth transition in the event that the initial senior appraiser retires, dies, or moves on. The firm is in place and prepared to provide the next appraisal, likely with a qualified business appraiser already known by the clients.

Finally, in the event that the parties become dissatisfied with the business appraisal firm that has been retained, the option remains to select another appraiser or firm for future appraisals.

IS YOUR BUY-SELL AGREEMENT "READY FOR TRIGGERING?"

In Chapter 2, I described the ideal time to sell a business or your interest in a business as:

- When the business is ready for sale.
- When the stock market is rising and the outlook is favorable.
- When the industry is hot.
- When low-cost financing is available.
- When irrational buyers abound.
- When the shareholders are ready to sell.

Again, these conditions will almost never all coincide for a given company at a given time. Given the lack of perfect coincidence, it is necessary and appropriate to be working to have your company in the best possible position to sell at any time. Only then will your business be ready when a reasonable opportunity comes along or you find that it is necessary or desirable to sell.

Unfortunately, in my experience, many, if not most companies are not "ready for sale" when they are ultimately sold, and their owners leave money on the table, sometimes substantial amounts, as a result.

But this is a book about buy-sell agreements, isn't it? What will conditions be like when your buy-sell agreement is triggered? Is your agreement "ready for triggering?" The reality is that you have little ability to predict when a buy-sell agreement will be triggered. Trigger events are unpredictable regarding who will be involved and when they will occur. Will the company be "ready for sale" when the trigger event occurs? If you are selling, will you obtain an optimal price? If you are remaining with the company and buying, will the purchase be affordable and reasonable? Is there a reasonable valuation mechanism? Are the other terms of the agreement reasonable to all parties? Given the lack of predictability of triggering events, it is necessary and appropriate to have your buy-sell agreement in place and "ready for triggering" all of the time.

However, in my experience, many, if not most buy-sell agreements have not received appropriate owner and advisor attention. The agreements are simply not ready for triggering when trigger events occur. The results are often dissatisfying for one or all parties, and frequently they are disastrous.

> **My challenge to you is to review your buy-sell agreement in the context of the information in this book. Be sure that your agreement is "ready for triggering" when the next trigger event occurs.**

CHAPTER NINETEEN

PETE AND SAM REPRISE

Pete:	"Well, Sam, we've covered a lot of ground in the last few hours."
Sam:	"We sure have. I didn't have any idea there were so many moving parts to a good buy-sell agreement."
Pete:	"Right. Let's recap what we've learned about your buy-sell. I do this in the most positive sense, because problems or issues identified can be addressed."
Sam:	"Let's hear my action list."
Pete:	"We've learned the following, at least:

- Your buy-sell agreement is a fixed-price agreement that was last looked at about eight years go.

- The price, or value, of the company in your agreement is $6 million, which was set eight years ago. But your business is worth maybe $20 million.

- There's a paragraph in your agreement that describes a process to update the price. But we know that the paragraph does not address all the defining elements we've learned about.

- The agreement does not address what happens if a shareholder gets divorced, and you indicated this could be an issue in the future.

- The company has life insurance of $2 million on our life and on George's, but that falls far short of the value of your interests of $7 or $8 million.

- There's no life insurance on the lives of William and Don, and their 10% interests are worth something close to $2 million each.

- The note the company would issue if it had to buy stock from any of the owners is completely unsecured. That's favorable for the company but risky for any selling stockholder. And, the interest rate isn't clearly specified, so there could be confusion there."

Sam:	"Other than that, Mrs. Lincoln, how was the play?"
Pete:	"As I've said before, these issues are not uncommon. And they can be fixed, either in a revision or rewrite of your buy-sell agreement."
Sam:	"How do we get started?"

Pete:	"For starters, begin talking to each other. I'd recommend that you share this book with George, Peter, and Don. Be sure to get your key advisors involved. You will be surprised at the perspectives they can provide if you ask them about the issues raised in this book. Once you've agreed on the business points of your buy-sell agreement, your attorney can draft the agreement you need. But you'll all have to read it and give the attorney your feedback to get the agreement finalized."
Sam:	"I'm pretty excited to get this process underway. We do have a bomb in our corporate yard – our buy-sell agreement! It is past time to get rid of it and to install an agreement that will work reasonably for all sides if something happens in the future."
Pete:	"Good luck! Be sure to have your key professionals read the agreement and give their comments. Once you change the agreement, it will likely be in place for a long time, so it is worth the investment to gain their perspectives. Above all, have your business appraiser read all of the language pertaining to the valuation process. That language will be tested in the first appraisal. You can fix it if there's an issue. Then you will all know it will work going forward, and the appraisal firm will appreciate being written into the agreement."
Sam:	"Sounds like a lot of work."

Pete: "Well, it does involve some work. What I can tell you is, regardless of the effort now, it will be easier, more productive, and more enjoyable than attempting to resolve the mess you would have if your current agreement were to be triggered. You can know your buy-sell agreement will work without triggering it."

Sam: "Wish us luck!"

Pete: "Break a leg!"

CHAPTER TWENTY

PROCESS-BUSTING VALUATION ISSUES

This is not a book about how to value businesses. There are many books that address that topic, even some of mine. However, there are at least five valuation issues that can blow a buy-sell agreement process completely out of the water. I have seen each of the issues in disputed valuation processes where there have been disagreements over:

⊙ The appropriate level of value

⊙ Embedded capital gains for asset holding entities

⊙ Tax-affecting of earnings in tax pass-through entities

⊙ Marketability (or illiquidity) discounts applied to controlling interest valuations

⊙ Key person discounts

The Appropriate Level of Value

We discussed the first process-busting issue, the appropriate level of value, in Chapter 14 so you are not only familiar with this issue already, but you know the best way to avoid having it arise in your valuation process. Remember, I recommend the *Single Appraiser, Select Now and Value Now* process described in Chapter 17. If you adopt this process, any misunderstandings will be discovered in the first appraisal, and your agreement can be fixed before a trigger event occurs.

This leaves four additional process-busting issues. Again, each of these issues should be avoided if you adopt the *Single Appraiser, Select Now and Value Now* valuation process for your buy-sell agreement.

Embedded Capital Gains in Asset-Holding Entities

If your business is primarily an asset-holding entity and there is substantial appreciation in the assets at the time of a valuation process, there is room for disagreement over the treatment accorded this issue by different business appraisers. The basic question is, of course, the appropriate treatment of any embedded capital gains that might exist relating to the appreciated assets.

Embedded capital gains exist when the market value of assets exceeds their book values on the books of entities. For example, if a company holds a single asset with a market value of $100 and a book value of $50, there is an embedded gain of $50 inside the entity. If the asset is sold, the capital gain will be triggered and due as a federal and, perhaps, state tax liability.

The embedded gains question from a valuation standpoint is the appropriate treatment of the gain. Is it a liability for valuation purposes or not? The potential disagreement is different whether your entity is a C corporation or a tax pass-through entity.

C Corporations

There are still quite a number of asset holding companies in existence that have retained the C corporation form of organization. Many of these entities are real estate holding entities. There are a significant number of C corporations that hold substantial amounts of appreciated real estate or securities. Let me illustrate the issue in a simple example. Assume the following:

⊛ A C corporation holds real estate with a current market value of $10 million. This has been determined by an independent real estate appraiser with excellent credentials and knowledge of the market where the real property is located.

- The book value of the real estate is $1 million, so there is an embedded capital gain of $9 million inside the company.

- There are no other assets or liabilities on the books of the company, so the book value of shareholders' equity is $1 million.

- The federal tax rate on embedded capital gains in C corporations is 40% and there are no state taxes on capital gains.

- The buy-sell agreement calls for two appraisers initially to provide appraisals of the business. If their conclusions are within 10% of each other, the price for purposes of the agreement is the average of the two conclusions.

- Two business appraisers have been retained, one by the company and the other by the estate of a deceased owner. The deceased owner held 20% of the stock.

- The buy-sell agreement is clear that no marketability or minority interest discounts are to be applied by the selected appraisers.

- Both appraisers have accepted the underlying real estate appraisals and have been asked to provide their opinions of the fair market value of the equity of the business.

Unfortunately, the appraisers' conclusions are not within 10% of each other:

- The first appraiser found that the net asset value of the business, after writing up the real estate to its fair market value, was $10 million, and that the value of the deceased owner's 20% share was $2 million. He did not consider the embedded capital gain of $9 million in his appraisal.

- The second appraiser stated that the embedded capital gain was a real liability of the company and that it should be considered dollar for dollar in the appraisal. She created an embedded capital gain liability of $2.6 million (40% times the gain of $9 million) and concluded that the net asset value was $6.4 million ($10 million minus $3.6 million). The estate's 20% interest was therefore worth only $1.28 million.

$2 million is 56% greater than $1.28 million, so the agreement calls for a third appraiser who will, presumably, agree with one of the two appraisers or somehow split the difference. This buy-sell agreement is busted.

What is the correct treatment of embedded capital gains in asset holding companies? Appraisers and courts have disagreed. I have taken the position that in the context of fair market value determinations, embedded capital gains in C corporation asset holding entities are real liabilities and should be deducted, dollar-for-dollar, in appraisals. I wrote an article on the subject. You may want your advisors to read it before you sign your agreement.[5]

A great deal of confusion has been raised over tax-affecting in the federal gift and estate tax arena, where fair market value is the standard of value. The confusion arose following the repeal of the General Utilities doctrine in 1987, which eliminated the potential for liquidating dividends for C corporations and created the embedded tax issue.

Additional confusion has been created in the arena of determinations of fair value in state statutory dissenters' rights and oppression cases.

If you stick with economics, I believe you will agree that if you have a C corporation asset-holding entity with substantial appreciated assets, you will want your appraiser(s) to tax-affect embedded capital gains.

Tax Pass-Through Entities

With tax pass-through entities, the question is the same. Should appraisers tax-affect embedded capital gains in tax pass-through entities? The short answer to this question, in my opinion, is no in most instances. When an

---

5   Mercer, Z. Christopher, "Embedded Capital Gains in C Corporation Asset Holding Companies," *Valuation Strategies*, November/December 1998.

asset is sold within a tax pass-through entity, the tax liability relating to any embedded capital gain becomes a pass-through liability of the owners (shareholders, partners, or members). However, other appraisers may disagree or just not know.

On the technical side of things, owners of tax pass-through entities have a separate basis for their investments outside the entities than the inside basis of the underlying assets. Assuming that distributions from sales of appreciated assets occur in the same tax year as gains are realized, holders of interests in tax pass-through entities will realize the expected economics of their investments if they pay for interests based on market values of assets without considering embedded capital gains. Sellers who sell based on consideration of embedded capital gains lose some of all of the benefit of their investment.

My advice as to the appropriate consideration of embedded capital gains for tax pass-through entities is that appraisers should not tax affect the gains in valuations for buy-sell agreements.

You may want to discuss this issue with your tax advisor and let him or her walk you through examples of what happens to buyers or sellers under varying assumptions about embedded gains.

Tax-Affecting Earnings in Tax Pass-Through Entities

Some appraisers believe S corporations are inherently more valuable than C corporations. They say, in effect, that since there is no corporate-level tax on earnings, the earnings should not be tax-affected for valuation purposes.

Other appraisers, like me, believe S corporations should be valued as if they were C corporations. Earnings (and those of other tax pass-through entities) should, therefore, be taxed at full corporate rates prior to capitalization in the valuation process.

The issue arises because there is a real economic benefit to being a tax pass-through entity relative to being a C corporation, and particularly if there are regular distributions of earnings. For purposes of this oversimplified discussion, assume that the federal corporate and individual tax rates are each 40%, and there are no state taxes. Assume also that before any taxes are paid, a C corporation and an otherwise identical S corporation earn $100 per year.

- The C corporation must pay $40 in federal income taxes, leaving $60 in the corporation to either distribute or to retain to support growth.

- The S corporation must pay no federal income taxes. However, the $100 of income is "passed through" to its owners, who in turn must pay their personal taxes on that income. In our example and in real life, the great majority of the time, the S corporation will write checks to its owners in an amount totaling $40 to pay their taxes. This leaves $60 in the corporation to either distribute or to retain to support growth.

The C corporation and S corporation are each left with $60 of retained earnings after writing checks to the IRS and the shareholders, respectively. It is, therefore, my opinion that there is no divergence of value between S and C corporations *at the level of the enterprise.* The benefit of the S corporation lies in its effect *at the shareholder level.*

The difference between C and S corporations arises when distributions are made by the C corporation or distributions in excess of those necessary to pay taxes are made by the S corporation.

- If the C corporation pays a dividend of, say, the $60 of after-tax earnings, its shareholders will pay a tax on dividends of, let's assume 20%. The tax paid by the individual stockholders, therefore, totals $12, and they have an after-tax benefit of $48.

⊙ If the S corporation distributes its $60 of after-tax earnings, its shareholders will pay no more taxes, and the after-tax benefit is therefore $60.

Since $60 (S) is greater than $48 (C), one argument suggests S corporations are worth more than C corporations. Another argument suggests that since S corporations pay no federal income taxes, they are worth more than C corporations. Both arguments are wrong. Once again, I have written about this issue, and you may want your advisors to take a look at the references.[6]

My recommendation is that if your business is housed in a tax pass-through entity, your buy-sell agreement should state that it is to be valued as if it were a C corporation. Here is why, using the example above. Assume that the appropriate multiple for valuation purposes is 10 times the after-tax earnings for the C corporation:

⊙ The C corporation is valued at $600 (i.e., 10 times after-tax earnings of $60). The shareholders get a 10% "earnings yield" on their investment at this valuation.

⊙ If the S corporation is also valued as if it were a C corporation, its value is also $600 (i.e., 10 times the after-tax earnings of $60), and its shareholders also get a 10% "earnings yield."

Now consider the alternative argument. If the S corporation is valued at 10 times after federal tax ($0) earnings of $100, then its value is $1,000, and not $600. If you happen to be a seller under your buy-sell agreement, you would get your share of $1,000. You would be happy, because you would get a lot more money than your share of $600 would represent.

---

6   Mercer, Z. Christopher, and Harms, Travis W., Chapter 10: Application of the Integrated Theory to Tax Pass-Through Entities," *Business Valuation: An Integrated Theory, 2nd Ed.* (John Wiley & Sons: 2007).

Mercer, Z. Christopher, "Are S Corporations Worth More Than C Corporations?," *Business Valuation Review*, September 2004.

The remaining owners might not be so happy. They still have to pay taxes of $40, so the S corporation has only $60 left. Their "earnings yield" is only 6%, which is a lot less than the expected 10% in the example.

If you know you will always be the seller – and you had better be the first seller – then perhaps you would want your S corporation valued without tax-affecting earnings. I say you had better be the first seller because if you were not, everyone else would figure out your game and it wouldn't work anymore. And, you would lose by overpaying to the first seller.

Again, my recommendation is that your buy-sell agreement should make it clear to future appraisers that your company is to be valued as if it were a C corporation. My company is an S corporation that has an employee stock ownership plan. I sold some of my stock to it a few years ago. Our appraisal was prepared as if we were a C corporation, as are the recurring annual appraisals that form the basis for our buy-sell agreement. Need I say more?

Marketability (or Illiquidity) Discounts Applied to Controlling Interests

Many buy-sell agreements with valuation processes provide guidance suggesting that appraisers should apply no discounts because of the minority nature of any holding and that there should be no discount for the lack of marketability of shares. The purpose of this guidance is to attempt to lead to a financial control level of value (see Chapter 14), and to ensure that minority interests are not discounted for their lack of marketability.

There are appraisers who still apply a so-called "marketability discount" to controlling interests of businesses. They sometimes use a different label, like illiquidity, but the effect is the same.

There is no theoretical basis for a marketability or illiquidity discount applicable to controlling interests in businesses. I wrote an article on this topic because of confusion in the appraisal profession.[7] You may want to suggest that your advisors read it before you sign your buy-sell agreement or while you are in the process of updating it.

Suffice it to say that if two appraisers value a business at $1,000 each and one takes a 25% illiquidity discount (or a discount by some other name that accomplishes the same thing), you will have a valuation dispute.

Key Person Discounts

It is indisputable that some owners are more important to a business than others. The term used in the valuation literature to describe this concept was called, historically at least, the "key man" discount. Now we use the term "key person."

In practice, it is appropriate to assess the riskiness of earnings in the discount rate. If there is a key person in a business, this may be an element of specific company risk that appraisers may appropriately take into account. What I am objecting to in this example, however, is the application of a nebulous and unsupported key person discount that lacks specific reasoning and support. Again, two appraisers could value a corporation at $1,000. If one applies a key person discount of 25% based solely on unsupported judgment, a valuation dispute is likely to become the result.

According to prevailing business valuation standards (see Chapter 14), any valuation premium or discount must be described and supported, and the rationale for its application must be stated.

If you are a key person and you know you will always be a buyer in buy-sell agreement transactions, this concept of a key person discount might not bother you. But you may well be a seller one day. That's no time for a big surprise in valuation.

---

7   Mercer, Z. Christopher, "Are Marketability Discounts Applicable to Controlling Interests in Private Companies?," *Valuation Strategies*, November/December 1997.

ONE FINAL CHALLENGE

As I said at the beginning of this chapter, this is not a book on how to value companies. But most of the valuation disputes I have seen regarding buy-sell agreements relate, directly or indirectly, to one of the five process-busting issues discussed in this chapter, as well as the levels of value issues covered in Chapter 14.

Let me conclude by saying problems with any or all of these issues can be eliminated by following the advice of this book. For most successful privately owned or family businesses, the best valuation process for their buy-sell agreements is the use of the *Single Appraiser, Select Now and Value Now* process outlined in Chapter 17.

If you go through the valuation process at the time you set up your buy-sell agreement initially – or now, if you revise your agreement based on material in this book – then your selected appraiser will provide an initial appraisal. Believe me, if any of these problems or any of the others I have mentioned are present, they will almost certainly be apparent when the appraiser provides an initial draft for your consideration. Then, you can revise the agreement to fix any problems before they arise. We end as we began: *You can know your buy-sell agreement will work without triggering it!*

> My final challenge to you is to take action on your buy-sell agreement now. You have the tools. You have the professional resources, or you can get them. And I hope you have the motivation. The risks are real, but they are avoidable. Just do it!

About the Author

Chris Mercer is the founder and CEO of Mercer Capital, one of the leading business appraisal and investment banking firms in the nation. Chris has been valuing businesses – and helping people buy and sell them – for more than 30 years.

Chris, a prolific writer, has authored eight books and more than 100 articles. Two of his recent books – *Business Valuation: An Integrated Theory, 2nd Edition* (with Travis W. Harms) and *Buy-Sell Agreements: Ticking Time Bombs or Reasonable Resolutions?* – highlight the breadth of his knowledge and experience, ranging from densely theoretical to highly practical. Chris is skilled at distilling complex ideas and concepts into understandable words and pictures.

Chris has served on the boards of several closely held or family businesses and on the board of one public company.

A much sought-after speaker, Chris lives in Memphis, Tennessee, with his wife, Ashley. They have five children between them: Amanda, Katherine, Katherine, Margaret, and Zeno. They also have two cats and two dogs, and they escape to their beach home in Destin, Florida, whenever possible.

Contact Chris:
mercerc@mercercapital.com
www.linkedin.com/in/zchristophermercer
901.685.2120 (p)

Articles Available for Reprint

Some of the content of this book has been summarized in short, readable articles. These articles are available for republication in your industry or business magazine, newsletter, or e-letter. You can review the articles at www.buysellagreementsonline.com.

You are welcome to publish the articles individually or in a series. We ask that you provide the following attribution at the end of each article that is published.

> Z. Christopher Mercer, ASA, CFA, ABAR is the CEO and founder of Mercer Capital, a national business valuation and investment banking firm. He is also the author of *Buy-Sell Agreements for Closely Held and Family Business Owners: How to Know Your Agreement Will Work Without Triggering It.* He can be reached at 901.685.2120 or mercerc@mercercapital.com.

Public Speaking

One of the greatest benefits of writing books has been the opportunity to speak to groups of business owners, financial planners, attorneys, accountants, and business appraisers. It is a pleasure to share experiences that can help others. Increasingly, accountants, wealth management professionals, financial service firms, industry associations, and family offices are organizing opportunities to bring messages from this book to business owners.

If you own a business or advise business owners and want to learn more about booking me to speak to your group, contact me (mercerc@mercercapital. com) or Barbara Walters Price (priceb@mercercapital.com). We can both be reached at 901.685.2120.

I can also provide the content in webinar format in the event that your group is scattered or if you are between normally scheduled meetings or conferences.

Z. Christopher ("Chris") Mercer, ASA, CFA, ABAR
901.685.2120 (p)
mercerc@mercercapital.com
www.buysellagreementsonline.com

Afterword

Throughout this book, I have challenged business owners to look at and to take charge of their buy-sell agreements. At this point, let me make the challenge even more personal.

I am one of the early Baby Boomers and a business owner, as well. I have tried to take my own advice. I have sold a significant portion of my stock in Mercer Capital to an employee stock ownership plan (ESOP). The ESOP is the most likely buyer for my remaining interest and that interest is subject to a workable buy-sell agreement.

Many readers of this book are also Baby Boomers. My next book will be designed to help with business transitions that are coming. Your business may not be as valuable as you would like, and it may not be ready for sale. Nevertheless, we will all transition our businesses.

Whether you or your business are ready for a transition right now, or you are working to get ready for that eventuality, my challenge to you is to commit to reviewing and revising your buy-sell agreement. Stuff happens in the life of businesses, including yours. You had better be sure that you, your family, the other shareholders, and the business are ready. You can know your buy-sell agreement will work without triggering it. Get the help you need. Call me or email me. I can help, or help you find someone who can.

Z. Christopher ("Chris") Mercer, ASA, CFA, ABAR
901.685.2120 (p)
mercerc@mercercapital.com
www.buysellagreementsonline.com

BUY-SELL
AGREEMENTS
for Closely Held and Family Business Owners

Do you know somebody who could benefit from reading *Buy-Sell Agreements for Closely Held and Family Business Owners?* It is the perfect gift for owners of all businesses, their families, directors, and advisors.

_____ copies @ $29.95 each = $ _____

(plus shipping :: $5.00 for first book, $2.00 for each add'l)

Orders of 10 or more copies qualify for quantity pricing. Call or email Chris Mercer (mercerc@mercercapital.com) or Barbara Walters Price (priceb@mercercapital.com) at 901-685-2120 for information.

Full Name _____

Company _____

Mailing Address _____

City, State _____ Zip _____

Phone _____ Email _____

Check enclosed payable to Peabody Publishing, LP in the amount of: $ _____

To order via credit card: (Circle One)   Visa   Master Card   Amex

Credit Card # _____ Exp. Date _____

Name on Card _____

Signature _____

Mail or fax completed order form and payment to:
Peabody Publishing, LP
5100 Poplar Avenue, Suite 2600, Memphis, TN 38137
901.685.2120 (p) » 901.685.2199 (f)

To order online, visit
www.buysellagreementsonline.com or www.mercercapital.com

BUY-SELL
AGREEMENTS
for Closely Held and Family Business Owners

Do you know somebody who could benefit from reading *Buy-Sell Agreements for Closely Held and Family Business Owners?* It is the perfect gift for owners of all businesses, their families, directors, and advisors.

_____ copies @ $29.95 each = $ _____

(plus shipping :: $5.00 for first book, $2.00 for each add'l)

Orders of 10 or more copies qualify for quantity pricing. Call or email Chris Mercer (mercerc@mercercapital.com) or Barbara Walters Price (priceb@mercercapital.com) at 901-685-2120 for information.

Full Name _____

Company _____

Mailing Address _____

City, State _____ Zip _____

Phone _____ Email _____

Check enclosed payable to Peabody Publishing, LP in the amount of: $ _____

To order via credit card: (Circle One)   Visa   Master Card   Amex

Credit Card # _____ Exp. Date _____

Name on Card _____

Signature _____

Mail or fax completed order form and payment to:
Peabody Publishing, LP
5100 Poplar Avenue, Suite 2600, Memphis, TN 38137
901.685.2120 (p) » 901.685.2199 (f)

To order online, visit
www.buysellagreementsonline.com or www.mercercapital.com

CPSIA information can be obtained at www.ICGtesting.com
Printed in the USA
LVOW070507040113

314303LV00002B/6/P